MW00427509

MONTESSORI TODDLER DISCIPLINES

HOW TO TALK SO YOUR CHILDREN WILL LISTEN: A SURVIVAL GUIDE TO LIFE FOR MOTHERS AND FATHERS

By

Susy Callory

This document is geared towards providing exact and reliable information with regards to the topic and issue covered. The publication is sold with the idea that the publisher is not required to render accounting, officially permitted, or otherwise, qualified services. If advice is necessary, legal or professional, a practiced individual in the profession should be ordered.

- From a Declaration of Principles which was accepted and approved equally by a Committee of the American Bar Association and a Committee of Publishers and Associations.

In no way is it legal to reproduce, duplicate, or transmit any part of this document in either electronic means or in printed format. Recording of this publication is strictly prohibited and any storage of this document is not allowed

TABLE OF CONTENTS

INTRODUCTION

Have you ever had a kid or a toddler who you talk to and repeat the same things to over and over again but he still doesn't listen, he still repeats the same kinds of mistakes? It almost feels as though your child is saying to you, "Momma, please stop being a nag!", right? And I am sure you have seen other people whose children listen to them when they talk. This is not to say you are doing a bad job as a parent, you are putting in your best, I am very sure of that. But let me tell you something here, your kids can and want to listen to you. They just need to understand what you are saying and they want you to understand what they are saying too. So, raising children that listen to you is something we are going to learn in this book.

Montessori toddler disciplines is a book you would love to read, that I can assure you. Why? You may ask me. From my years of experience, there is one thing that I know very common with parents, especially the new one. We all want to give our children the best upbringing possible. This is because we want them to have an upstart in life. We do not want them to be lagging behind among other children. So, we always want to give it our best shots. This book helps you to do just that. Over the years, the Montessori method has been proven to teach children to grow and become excellent children without external pressures. In this book, we bring it home. We learn how to apply the Montessori method while raising the children at home and also in school. It's going to be an awesome read, I can assure you.

Raising children has always posed a great deal of problems for parents and guardians. As much as we love and want the best for them, we just do not know how to go about it. We simply cannot afford to make mistakes in their upbringing; that could be very disastrous. Childcare and training is a very dicey subject; you could think you're doing the best you could but the results are very heartbreaking; this very thought causes parents and guardians to fret.

Children, on the other hand, are tough to handle- or so they seem. They want to be everywhere, do everything at the same time. This could, no doubt, threaten a person's sanity. There is just so much energy than you know what to do with. Well, what if I told you that there's a way to put that energy to good use?

Children take in a lot of information, more than we imagine. They see, hear and feel, and even though they don't understand at that point, the information has a way of shaping their lives. Imagine subjecting your wards to educative exercises while making them think they are playing. Well, basically, they are playing, they're just learning while at it. It could be a game, a play, anything that screams fun, at the end, you'll have a satisfied and educated ward. This is what the Montessori system offers.

The term "Montessori" was named after the founder of the system, Dr. Maria Montessori; and Italian physician, educator, and women's rights activist. Dr. Montessori first worked with what she called "phrenestatic children"; these were children with mental disabilities or illnesses. From here on, she began to develop an interest in the activities of teaching and education. When she was appointed as co-director of the Orthophrenic school -an institute that would train teachers on how to deal with mentally disabled children- in 1900, she developed a curriculum and materials which would be used to train these children.

Later on, she applied this curriculum on mainstream children, most of whom were always left on their own when their parents went off to work. It was observed that children have an innate need to want to order their environment, be in control of what goes on around them and try things out for themselves. So, these children were introduced to environments and activities that encouraged them to learn at their own pace. These activities were designed to suit the children allowing them to choose what interested them and hence, support their natural development and there were instances of spontaneous repetition of these activities which increased their level of success.

This inclusive system of education proved to be more effective than other systems. It eventually became widespread, gaining acceptance in more and more schools over the years, with impressive success rates. Because of this, more efficient ways of handling children in the crucial formative years of their lives were developed and the children subjected to the Montessori curricula proved to perform better at academics than their peers.

The Montessori method does more than enhance only the academic life of children; it instills strong leadership skills and builds interpersonal intelligence, gives them the independence toddlers crave. The activities included cover all the bases, thus, educating the total man. Needless to say, this method can and should be employed by parents and guardians.

At a Montessori school, your child would be placed in an environment constructed to encourage creativity and, even with the presence of a supervisor, self-reliance, there would be time assigned for different activities, all tailor-made to suit the child. At home, you could also set-up this "environment", it could be a room, a small portion of the house or even a whole house, whichever works for you.

Children are naturally and continually craving for knowledge; their world is new to them so they want to explore. The Montessori system provides an environment that supports and encourages them to reach their maximum potential. This book covers a multitude of possible questions and sticky situations for parents and guardians concerning childcare and training and will help you raise a human being you would be proud of.

APPROACH FOR THE MONTESSORI GUIDE

The Montessori exercises are designed to meet the needs of children in a specific age grade, so, for the purpose of this book, we will be focused on toddlers. As earlier stated, every aspect of the Montessori curriculum is designed to support the child's development, so, there is sync between the child's natural predilections and the provided activities. Children should not be forced to take up activities or indulge in games they have shown no interest in, this will provide a negative result. Parents and guardians should understand that children, toddlers, are still trying to understand the world they find themselves in, hence, their high level of curiosity. This being the case, they could be coaxed into certain activities but should never be forced if they do not want to indulge. The idea is for them to learn at their own pace, they could respond at the very beginning or well into the training, patience would go a long way in getting the desired results.

In this chapter, we would be seeing safe approaches to the Montessori guide

Independence.

The basic aim of the Montessori curriculum is to make the child able to "stand on his own feet", develop the ability to do certain things on his or her own. This is achieved by actually letting them handle themselves. Let them prepare themselves for bed on their own from time to time, let them prepare themselves for school, you could peep in and check on their progress while they do so without overly alerting them to it, let them choose what they want to do for a fun time out, you could even ask them to rinse out their dishes after a meal. This would make them feel trusted and capable and, in the long run, would make them self-reliant and each time they complete these tasks successfully, their self-esteem goes up a notch or two.

Observation.

Watching your child or ward play is very easy, and I daresay pleasurable for the parents to do. We could spend an eternity just watching them interact with the world around them, having the time of their lives. There is thus heart melting joy in seeing them so happy, we sometimes wish we could crystallize those moments so they would last forever. Well, this one approach would prove beneficial for your children or wards as well as relaxing for the parents and guardians. In simply watching, really observing, we could see things in our children we might have missed. How he/she seriously studies flowers or how she/he is attracted to bright colors, little things like that. This simple act could go a long way in helping you to meet the needs of those little ones. Why, it was how Dr. Maria Montessori started out, watching and observing, taking notes. So just sit back and really pay attention without any preconceived notions or thoughts on how they should be rather than how they are at the moment.

Learn to play “Follow the leader”.

"Follow the children, they will show you what they need to do, what they need to develop in themselves and what area they need to be challenged in. The aim of the children who persevere in their work with an object is certainly not to "learn"; they are drawn to it by the needs of their inner life, which must be recognized and developed by its means." - Dr. Maria Montessori.

So, now you have watched your child or ward and picked out traits peculiar to them. What did you find out? Does he want to climb over something all the time? Does she tend to always bang on something? You should provide them with materials and activities that help them develop this part of themselves, chances are they will either grow with or out of the habit. Just stand back and watch them be. Do not be too restrictive, give them what they need and stay at a safe distance to keep an eye on them, if they don't seem to be harming themselves or others around them, then let them just have fun. Try not to help. You'll be building their sense of independence as well as letting them explore themselves and who they are, which is very crucial in this formative stage of their lives. As parents or guardians, knowing when to step in, when to turn a blind eye and when to let go is very important; it could strengthen or strain your relationship with your child and ward respectively and it could put a dent in their self-reliance. Give the little ones a sense of freedom of choice, observe and fill their needs, make them feel free to ask questions then explain in the best way possible, no matter how awkward or inappropriate the question is, NEVER SHY AWAY FROM ANSWERING THEM. Chances are, those questions will still plague them and finding the answers will become a need, you may not like how they go about finding their answers, it may even turn out to be really harmful. It would be a lot safer if you, as the parent or guardian, are able to control the situation, their curiosity would be fed and they will know only what they need to know for the time being.

Children are clumsy creatures, they tend to spill or drop things, sometimes unintentionally and other times, just for the fun of it. But hey, they do not know any better, so there is really no need to raise your voice at them in such situations. It could be really frustrating so you should try a lot of patience. Try getting them to understand their mistake, let us see a common situation.

Your child is playing with water colors, but decides at some point to paint his table instead of his coloring book. Instead of raising your voice or yelling at them, you could try “honey, the table is not to be painted on. You don’t want to ruin it, do you?” -you get the picture? You could even ask them to get a rag and wipe it clean; you would be playing on their need to want to do things on their own as well as teaching them responsibility. Instead of yelling or abruptly reprimanding them when they do something wrong, explain to them why such things should not be done. Scolding your children or wards would make them shrink away from you and give a sense of insecurity which would prove very unhealthy for them.

“The educator’s first duty is to watch over the environment, and this takes precedence over all the rest. Its influence is indirect, but unless it is well done, there will be no effective and permanent results of any kind, physical, spiritual or intellectual.” – Maria Montessori.

From the beginning of this book, we have stressed the importance of a child's environment for his development. The right environment for work is very crucial for the child, if it is dull and boring, the child is put off, if the color scheme is drab, they would prefer anywhere else to that place. The right environment is the springboard for the child to learn. Beautifully and systematically set up rooms and activities would attract the children and make them eager to explore.

According to Dr. Montessori "work is an activity which the child does, what many people would call play". This "work" is the way in which they find out who they are, so their work is their play and their play is their work, so, it is expedient that they have a comfortable "work environment" for maximum effectiveness. This environment also includes the parents and guardians, never leave your children or ward unattended for long, be present when you are needed but let them have full control of what they want to do.

Ever wonder how children pick up a language without having anyone teach them? This is because in those formative years they simply learn by absorbing everything in their environment, being a part of it. This is the phenomenon that gave birth to Dr. Montessori's "The Absorbent Mind". For this reason, it is very important to watch what you say or do to and around your children and wards, they may not be able to fully express themselves yet but you don't want them flicking the middle finger at you when they can. Thing is, they may not really understand what some of these things mean or how wrong they are, but because it's something they have seen or heard over time, it forms an integral part of who they are. They would begin to exhibit these things without so much as a thought to them. If they are being loud or noisy, say "keep your voice down" instead of "shut up", try "go to your room" instead of "get away", same message, different approaches. Whatever you wouldn't want your children or ward doing or saying, try not to do or say those things around them, these things have a way of coming around to bite you in the butt.

Know the difference between show and tell.

We tell our children and wards a lot of things, rights and wrongs, but what do they see you do? It looks a lot like the last approach but there's a twist. You see, we want our kids to be a certain kind of way, act in a certain kind of way, so we try to talk them into it, but how do we act? Do they see these same traits in us? This is very important as children are going to do what they see you do over what you tell them. So if you say "be kind", actually be kind, they are watching and learning.

Look them in the eyes.

Children are as human as they come, so, do not treat them less. Look them in the eyes when addressing them whether you are scolding or praising or simply instructing and when they are also talking to you. This shows them that they have your respect, they might not know the word, but they know the feeling. It also shows them that they have your complete attention. You like this act reciprocated, so be the first to give it.

Be in sync with your child or ward.

So you want your child or ward to learn a particular thing, but he does not seem to be getting a hang of it, well, let it go for a while. If you keep pushing, they would begin to feel frustrated, you might think you're doing them a favor, but you're breaking them and making them develop a certain fear and dislike for the said activity. If your child, however, is still bent on making it work, then let him. Just be with them, not ahead, not behind.

Ask nicely.

At this point, we have already established the evidence that the children should be allowed to do stuff around the house, what we have not talked about though, is how to achieve this. It is easier to make them do things because you're way older and you're the adult, but how effective is this approach? Children want to be treated as adults, they want to do what the adults are doing, whether they understand it or not, bossing them around could either make them obstinate. Try "inviting" them to do a thing or “suggest” that they do it. They would feel like they have a choice, and because you asked nicely, they would be happy to oblige.

SPECIFIC LANGUAGE RECOMMENDATIONS

Language is the fundamental point of difference between the human species and all others. Language lies at the root of that environment that we call civilization." – Dr. Maria Montessori.

Your relationship with your child is just like every human relationship. For it to thrive, healthy communication is very important. In communication, you are basically sending and receiving information to and from your child/ward. There are various kinds of information. Information can be visual, audio or in some other kinds of format. Hence, there are many types of communication, it can be verbal where words are communicated between parties or non-verbal where actions or body language are communicated between parties. Funny enough, the majority of human communication is non-verbal. Parent-child communication is not any different.

As parents or guardians, you need to realize that effective communication is one thing that should happen in your relationship with your children/ward. This is vital as your child is in his/her formative years of life. They need to know that they can trust you and rely on you. Communication builds trust, so you need to get it right. No pressures, I would be showing you specific language recommendations to make this possible.

Effective communication improves relationships. This is the same for parents and children. Once the child feels you are understanding him or her, he would relate with you more and this would lead to better interaction and relationships.

As much as children like to be independent, they also learn by observation, they love to copy what they see. In communication also, children learn by looking at how their parents communicate. Parents who are open in communicating usually have children who are more expressive. This would mean that you can imbibe good communication skills in your children by communicating with them often and also communicating around them regularly.

When you communicate well with your toddlers, this would benefit them for the rest of their lives. Everybody loves to be regarded and respected. Toddlers and children are no different. When you communicate with them often, it makes them feel you value and respect them. When you talk with and to them, it makes them feel you are showing them respect. Once a toddler feels he/she is heard and understood, his/her self-esteem receives a large boost.

Obedient children are more as a result of communicative parents. When you can communicate effectively with your toddlers, your children are more willing to do the things you tell them to do. They see reason in what you are telling them to do, they understand you and they do these things not only because you asked them to, but because they want to. Remember, they are independent.

Communication with toddlers can be very tricky, you have to know just the right things to say in the right situations and the things to avoid so as not to hurt their feelings. Here are a few tips on how to tread this slippery road.

- Ask and expect: The child's mind is always wandering, they could be on one project this moment then run away to play, the next. This is due to their need to explore anything and everything around them, so, when you ask a question or give and instruction, expect a response. When they wander off or begin to talk about something else, draw their attention back to the subject and, nicely but firmly, ask for a response.

- Children have spats with one another, it does not necessarily mean anyone involved is a troublemaker; humans and conflict are like wine and chocolate. However, what you do in these situations would go a long way in the development of the child. If your child or ward has a disagreement with another child, instead of settling the issue, guide them in resolving their problem. It instills social intelligence in everyone involved, teaching them that disagreements and misunderstandings can and should be solved by dialogue.

- It's really frustrating when children refuse to share; it causes a raucous and it seems like there is really no just way to settle it. So, Lisa wants to play with Chloe's doll but Chloe does not want to share. Lisa gets hurt and begins to wail but Chloe is set on her decision, it is her doll afterward. Instead of taking the doll from Chloe and handing it to Lisa, ask Chloe to share, if she refuses, let her be. Children are wired to think of themselves first but can be really giving when they want to. Find something else for Lisa to play with, then when Chloe is done, she will have the doll.

- Let your child or ward know that you understand them. When they are sad, instead of just assuming you know why, ask them about it. Prompt them to talk and listen without judging. Ask them why they feel the situation is making them sad, then you ask them what they would want to do about it.

- Always ask questions. At this point, we would have deduced the importance of asking your children or ward questions instead of jumping to your own conclusions. You might think you have a handle on what the problem is, but hearing them talk about it would give a fresh perspective. It would also give them an opportunity to vent and express themselves. This step would also make them feel like they could talk to you about any and everything, no matter how big or small it is.

- Never turn a blind eye to the feelings of your child or ward. When you have hurt them, whether you think they deserved it or not, acknowledge it and apologize. Explain why you did it and call a truce. Children are human beings too with real feelings and they are way more sensitive than the average adult, so the littlest things get to them.

- Call it as it is. Try not to lie to your child or ward; the truth is, they see what goes on around them and even though it does not seem like it, they know when you lie to them. In some cases, the toddler might not contradict you just because, but they know when you lie. This would cause them to distrust you because they would feel you always lie to them.

- Try to use the proper words for the right objects. Avoid slangs as much as possible; we don't want our toddlers picking up on wrong words now, do we?

HOW TO RAISE RESPONSIBLE AND CURIOUS TODDLERS

Training a child is not instinctive; care can be, but training is not. To train a child, you have to pay keen attention to the details that this child is constantly expressing. To raise a toddler is a whole lot of work; people actually stop working to focus on raising their kids, to show how important it is. It is not something you learn in a day. Every child grows differently, every child expresses himself differently and you must realize these differences while training your children. Schools also must put this in perspective; they don't all grow the same. Training is still necessary and how you imbibe this character into a toddler is what we would be discussing. Toddlers would eventually mature into adults, and the things they picked up while growing ultimately form them into the adult they would eventually become. That means the building blocks that are required for a person to grow and form into a successful individual are laid in his/her childhood. That's why it is very important that we pay attention to the important aspects of a child's life which would impact how the child grows.

How exactly do you get them to be responsible?

The years of a toddler (from 12-36 months) are the years of development in their cognitive, social, emotional development. It's that time in their growth where they want to touch, feel, engage everything. It's this time in their growth that they swallow everything around the house; they rip out the pages of the books they encounter; they want to paint and color walls—they just want to express their curiosity and their energy.

Inversely when you take something that belongs to your toddler and he/she flips, trying to reason with them at this point won't work; they just want what they want at that moment. The lower part of their brain—where a set of neurons responsible for their emotional outburst is located—takes over. These set of neurons is called the Amygdala. The Amygdala is an important part of the limbic system. The limbic system is responsible for your emotions and hormonal coordination. In kids, they don't know how to be logical when they are emotional; they have to grow up into these things—to learn how to control their emotions.

Your toddler doesn't have a skill called executive function and self-regulation skills; the child is like a loose cannon. This skill helps you focus attention, plan, remember instructions and multitask successfully. Your Toddler cannot yet reconcile the fact that whatever thing they might do has consequences that might harm them. They just want to have fun—they just want to express their curiosity and their energy. You might want to tell them over and again what you want them to do and use relatable examples; you have to paint in their mind that actions have consequences so that they do not run off thinking everything is all fun, they could be hurt in the future.

What shapes our brain? The experiences we encounter as we grow. Whenever you experience something new, your brain cells (neurons) are activated and begin to make connections with other neurons in the brain. This is how behavioral patterns are formed. The first time you went to school and the emotion that you got from it shaped you; the first time you drove, the first time you got robbed; all these experiences shaped you. That's how it is for your toddler—their experiences shape them, you need to create the best experience for their mind to thrive.

You must understand that more than what you say, your toddler would follow what you do. They are curious like that. They always want to do what they see beyond what you are saying. I mean, they even find it hard to understand some words you use. I remember a toddler asking me what "consequence" meant, I asked him what he thought it was and he said he thought it was some sort of computer—you get my point?

They would easily follow what you are doing than what you are saying. Those gestures help them understand what you are saying faster. The child would learn better when he or she sees examples that they can relate with. If you want them to do the dishes after a meal, teach them by examples, if you want them to pick up their toys and organize it, show them how to, if you want them to learn to share, do exactly that and you'd notice that they would want to participate most times as you cook, or shop, or clean, or wash—they easily follow your examples over what you say. If you say it and do the opposite, be sure your child would be confused.

Learn to assign things to them, things they can handle. Don't tell them to do things they can't handle. In the class, you can give them age appropriate tasks like "Todd you would be responsible for arranging your crayons properly". You can guide Todd through the process, patiently ensuring that he sticks to the plan. They would gradually form a responsibility towards that task and would eventually own it. Have chores clearly stated for them at home, maybe with the help of an older sibling but make sure they are engaged; maybe they get to arrange their toys, or organize their books, or help keep the dishes as the older sibling washes them. Examples in this context are the best teachers.

Repeat and repeat and repeat. Most times we think just saying it one time would suffice; I believe reality has taught us the truth. Don't assume your toddler knows and has heard, repeat over and again. You can colorfully create learning aids to help them remember the tasks you have given. They really need to learn to take the initiative. So, repeat, and repeat such that it becomes a rhyme stuck in their minds. One of my favorite songs to sing to my toddlers is the "brush your teeth" song. We composed the song in class and everyone does gestures as we sing along.

Every good job done deserves some praise. You know that feeling you get when you do something right and your boss gives you praise in front of everyone? Do you know what would follow? You would typically want to do more to get him to praise you more. Kids also feel the same way; you can see the blood rush through their face and the grin that follows when you praise them. So, praise them heavily for tasks completed. Don't withhold that praise! Let them have it, for every task they complete validate them in front of everyone; give them high fives and speak highly of the task. Now, when a kid does something you should not expect it to be perfect, even you didn't learn to ride a bike in two minutes, it took time, and so before they become experts, they would do things shabbily — still praise them for it. Validation is very important to their self-esteem and their confidence towards solving problems.

Apart from praising them, reward them, but don't over indulge. If you reward them too much they would think that for every action or task they complete, they would need to be rewarded and that can give them an entitlement mentality. You need to use the rewarding wisely. You can build a chart that has stars on it; for each task a kid completes, he or she would have the opportunity to move his/her star into a new box. This can be pretty rewarding for the toddler.

Consequences are real; they affect our everyday lives. This world works by cause and effect, it means whatever we do has an effect on existence. For every action we take, the impact can affect a person, two people, millions, the whole earth or even the universe. The consequence of not eating for days can be drastic, the consequence of not raising a properly trained child can be devastating; imagine the thousands of lives that would be affected if that child is not groomed properly. A child cannot be absorbed from the thought that consequences don't exist when he experiences these consequences himself and they are not pleasant. I had a toddler that liked to drink water from a puddle; he got infected with germs and fell sick. Toddlers are that energetic, they would want to see, feel, touch and taste everything that they see—that's how they would learn. Your job is to direct that energy to the right areas. We have had toddlers die because of little mistakes that we make like this.

According to Stanford Children's health injury is the leading cause of death in children and young adults. Approximately 12,000 children and young adults die as a result of injuries each year. Drowning is the leading cause of unintentional injury among children ages 1-4. These accidents occur in residential swimming pools and open water sites; children can drown in as little as one inch of water. Airway obstruction is also a leading cause of infant mortality in children under age 1. You really need to take this seriously because their lives might just be hanging on the balance.

How do you do this?

Spell the consequences clearly and in relatable terms; you can use learning aids like we outlined earlier. You can colorfully pass the message you want to pass to them and help them see the consequences of these actions and what it means. For instance, if you warn your toddler against not arranging his or her crayons, you would need to repeat it to them over and again, and if they default, look for ways to express disappointment and let them see the consequence of their actions—they would become conscious of the consequences of certain actions but it takes time, patience and intelligence. A toddler must come to learn that they would not get everything that they want, how they want it and when they want it. You are still the boss. These kids don't have the mental build to survive on their own; they don't know what delayed gratification is, they don't know what intelligent choices are, they are still too curios to know that a snake may not be a pet. These facts are reasons why you would not leave your toddler to make decisions for himself; you need to show them that they can't always get what they want especially when the thing they are asking would negatively impact them. They should also know that when they do something wrong, there would be consequences and this should be highlighted strongly.

If you correct a person, always give them the chance to change to see if what you told them was well received. That should be applied here too; when you teach a toddler a new lesson, give them time to grow into it, don't rush them if not they might miss the importance of the process and just do it to please you.

A toddler knows when you are not pleased with an action of his, if he sees that what he does hurts you, he might stop; but it's not enough to just stop an activity, you want to be sure that the toddler knows exactly why the task was given or why you corrected them; they really need to understand so that they can really benefit from the process.

Tom was a 2-year kid that was very aggressive to his friends, we sat him down and found out why he was doing that, he said he felt afraid and thought that these people were going to hurt him. He did not know how to handle anxiety and threats; so he responds with violence. When we corrected him, he had another fight but something was different, he felt very remorseful in comparison to other times he fought. What we did was that we brought him again, and spoke to him about how he could change and how we would work on his change together. We saw changes in Tom and it was amazing.

There is a story that helps me buttress this point: there was a man that watched a butterfly struggle to emerge from its cocoon. He watched how it struggled to set one wing free and when it did, it just hung down from the cocoon exhausted. The man pitied the butterfly and freed the second wing from the cocoon. He noticed that the butterfly could not flap both its wings; it could only use one wing. The wing that was incapacitated was the wing that he set free.

The struggle was to make the butterfly's wing strong enough to handle the air pressure, make it strong enough to flap as many times as it needed to fly. He thought he was helping the butterfly by cutting short the process, don't do that with your toddlers, allow them grow when you correct them. Patience in this case is a very important key to ensuring they grow.

Curiosity is the backbone of learning, it is the reason why you want to try out new things, and it is the reason why you enjoy a lecture above another lecture. Without curiosity life and learning would be bland and lackluster. Curiosity adds that special spice that gives life the spark we see. It is how people change, it is also how you teach an old dog new tricks; the reason why you can't teach an old dog new tricks is that the dog has seen everything that needs to be seen and many things have gone past fascinating it—but if you want an old dog to learn new tricks, get ready to get the dog curios.

Babies are born with this gift because they haven't had enough experience to knock out all the curiosity they have in stock. We really do not have to make the kids curious, we only harness this curiosity. We channel all their curios energy into very productive things. We have instances where curiosity went wrong; situations when the toddler puts things in his mouth that harm him, puts his hand in fire, or uses equipment that they don't know how it works. I remember certain news that was making rounds amongst that a toddler out of curiosity did take his father's documents and colored them, the dad took them thinking he was done with what his boss asked him to do and submitted a colorful work to his boss. The event was laughable but we can take all that colorful energy and channel it the right way.

What parents or trainers do is that they try to quench the curiosity—that is all shades of wrong, don't quench it, and rather let it soar in the right direction. That's where you come in, directing their curiosity and sharpening that curiosity because they need a whole lot.

How do you do that?

Give them more to work with. Don't keep them locked up in the house 24/7, take them to parks, travel on vacations to places they have never been to, allow their mind to feed on all the colors, all the lights, the sounds, just let their eyes do all the eating. Take them for walks in the evening, allow them to explore in their heads. This would help their curiosity remain nimble.

Let your child lead you; let your child's curiosity lead you; don't shove an interest down their throat, if your child has come to love a certain activity, watch them and help them flourish in that area. Their curiosity would be best channeled in that area where they have expressed interest. Get them materials to help that curiosity; visuals, auditory…anything that would ensure that they keep on learning and growing.

I am sure you have your own bag of questions because it is typical that you are asked weird questions—that's curiosity speaking. Questions like "why is water wet?" or, "where do babies come from" or "why do dogs have a tail?", that's why I encourage parents to be widely read so that they can at least provide answers for their kids' curiosity or at least guide them through the struggle. One of the worst things you would do would be to make them feel like their questions are not smart or not necessary; it can have a negative impact on their curiosity. You have to be patient like I said with answering their questions. Don't be afraid to let them know you do not have the answers to their questions but you could help them search it out if they could be patient.

One of the things you do not want to do to your kid is to lie to them. If you say you want to do something, make sure you do exactly as you said because they would remind you. When you say you would learn with them, make sure you actually learn with them. Using fiction and some unreal characters to entertain them is good but it could work for a few years or more, when you realize they found out that Santa isn't real, you can switch tools and begin using clearer tools to inspire them.

Use open ended questions. Most trainers/parents don't know how to use open ended questions to spark up a conversation or continue one. These questions are questions that can't be answered with yes or no, they are not questions that might register as right or wrong, they are questions that engage the mind more to think up more words than just giving a direct yes or no. Examples of some open ended questions: "What about math, do you not like?" "How was school today?" "What did your teacher say about your new hair?" The more the child is conscious that you would ask these questions, they would pay attention to details that they believe you might ask. You are simultaneously training their minds and channeling their curiosity.

You have to also pay keen attention to the environment of your child; you want them to be curios and creative? Make their environment look like it. A bland environment won't cut it. Use a lot of colors, mascots, icons, and crafts, make the environment as energetic as you want their minds to be. Then engage your kid in very educating games. There are games/activities that are known to boost cognitive abilities in kids and affect their ability to solve problems. Certain games also affect spatial intelligence and improve creativity. For instance, allowing them to build with Lego (under supervision, because you don't want anyone swallowing tiny pieces of Lego) is another way to engage their minds and curiosity. You can let them play with clay, pots, pans, crayons, boxes, arts and crafts etc.

Attention to detail is a skill parents/trainers need to have. You would not successfully train the child if you skim over very important detail. For instance, if you notice your child loves to play with dirt which could be harmful, you can stop him from doing that and create an alternative. Why? You don't want them to lose that spark. Don't discourage them from exploring; just monitor how they are expressing themselves.

MONTESSORI AND THE POSITIVE DISCIPLINES

Can I tell you something amazing? A lot of renown people today were actually schooled in Montessori-based schools. Isn't it interesting to note that the founders of Google, Sergey Brin and Larry Page, top music and fashion icon, Sean "Diddy" Combs, among others, were all educated using Montessori-based schools? Little wonder why they are so creative and successful in life. As you can see, Montessori education is a very important factor in success for your children.

When you want to select the program and discipline that your child should participate in, there are a lot of things to consider. Programs include daycare, pre-schools and home-schooling. Also, one thing to consider is the philosophy of education and educational approach the school uses. This is very vital to your decision. Styles of teaching abound in Montessori education. One thing is common though, they encourage independence in children, creativity, natural child development among others.

The Importance of Montessori Education for Children

Montessori education focuses on development at the earliest stages. Where other schools focus on passing knowledge, Montessori schools are concerned with development; self-development. The Montessori Method of educating was not just decided upon. Rather it was the end result of a lot of scientific research out into learning children. Montessori schools are of the opinion that it is better to 'show a child' than to 'tell a child'. In a Montessori setting, fundamental aspects of a child's life are worked on. Rather than simply teaching what can be forgotten, Montessori schools teach how to learn. Montessori education grooms a child to independence. With the rate at which the world is changing, Montessori education is fast changing from being labeled a privilege to a necessity. This is because a wider number of people are discovering its benefits and attaching fitting importance to it.

Here are some of the most widely known importance of Montessori Education.

Montessori Education Develops Mental Skills

Every aspect included in Montessori education has been deemed necessary and beneficial for developing children. In the developmental stages of children, if they are provided with the opportunity to think for themselves and explore their own capabilities with a trained teacher's guidance, the learning restraints are automatically lifted off them thereby allowing them to develop faster and healthier. Montessori education encompasses all levels of development a child should pass through.

Montessori Education Focuses on Practical More Than Theory

Montessori education deals with what students can see; it deals with what they can do. Their hands and minds are put to work which makes it an excellent all-rounder exercise. Both the physical and mental faculties are put to work. This continuous process of learning, observing, correcting, analyzing, and back to learning again is an unbeatable one. Children are taught resilience. They are taught to press forward and are rewarded with their own success.

Montessori Makes Use Of The 'Follow The Child' Approach

The 'Follow The Child' approach simply indicates that the speed at which new things are introduced is dependent on the child. The child is not forced to learn at the pace of others but at her own unique speed. This allows the child to develop as she would. Due to the fact that the child is not rushed, the trained teacher can discover her strengths and weaknesses. Montessori schools also mandate the cosmic curriculum that teaches the child in-depth things about the world they live in order to stir up curiosity and awe. The curiosity stirred increases their hunger to learn more.

Montessori Education Develops Social Skills

At Montessori schools, children's interactions with each other are closely guarded and guided. Montessori schools create a comfortable and homely atmosphere that allows children to interact with other children. The interactions can be purely social or achievement-driven. Such interactions can be collaborations. In the end, the aim of building social skills is actualized. Students are taught to collaborate and respect each other. A generation with children groomed to respect each other and be conscious of other people is a generation that moves forward.

Montessori schools build independence in children

In average school settings, children are taught to depend too much on the teacher. However, in the Montessori system, as children are encouraged to make their own decisions, they gain small measures of independence. The freedom given to them to analyze and tackle problems builds independence.

The Montessori Schools For All Types Students

Non-Montessori schools usually have problems dealing with special children. Special children have to be taken to schools that can understand their uniqueness. With the availability of Montessori education, such segregation is not necessary. The Montessori ideology is suitable and compatible with children of all abilities. Gifted children, as well as average children, will benefit immensely from the ideology. In the same vein, gifted above-average, and below-average children will benefit from Montessori education.

Montessori Education Improves the Ability to Learn

As mentioned before, Montessori education does not expect a child to just learn. There is a carefully mapped out plan on how the knowledge should be passed and how the child should be conditioned to receive it. Montessori education makes a child more receptive to learning. It simplifies the learning process. Children with learning difficulties will benefit tremendously from Montessori education. The trained teachers lay out the mapped course of action and allow their students to guide themselves along the path.

Montessori Focuses On Personal Development Of Each Child

The aim of the Montessori way of imparting knowledge is not pitting children against each other to see who performs best. Montessori schools do not compare students to other students. A child's improvement is not compared to another. Rather, the trained teacher works on each child to ensure that the child makes progress in regards to his previous performance and his alone. It is no secret that children develop differently. Due to this, comparing their progress at a particular stage is wrong and futile. A lot of factors come into place to affect a child's ability to learn. These factors are not the same in every child and so, it is pretty illogical to compare them.

Montessori Schools Build Self-Assessment

Montessori education has a child assess his or her own decisions. The ability to assess one's work brings them a step closer to making improvements. They can ask questions, reason differently, and form their own thought trains. That is what Montessori aims at. When they asses their own decisions, they can take it a step further and put corrections in place themselves.

Montessori Schools Give Students A Permanent Edge

In a 2006 Journal published by a US psychologist who carried out research on children, there was documented information on Montessori school children compared to systemic school children. It was discovered that children who attended Montessori schools had better-developed minds. They were more independent, solved problems more easily, and adapted quicker to new developments. They were also more emotionally experienced and could interact more intelligently. They were less likely to be found in trouble and related better with people.

Montessori schools are the only schools that allow a child to learn in the way best for him. Allowing a child to learn at his or her own unique pace works wonders.

Every adult that loves kids would want these kids to learn very strong principles, good character traits, good social skills and form into a fine adult. You would guide them towards the appropriate behavior and discipline. There is no one way to make a child disciplined because humans are wired differently, what could work for child 'A' may not work for child 'B'; you have to know what works for every child that comes around you.

I remember a kid; her name was Karen. Karen was always by herself and she found it very difficult to share with other kids, she won't also like to participate in class, I tried using my authority as an adult to lure her out of her shell; she came out, but she sat still and did nothing. I figured it was just more than a kid that was shy, something else was wrong. I started making efforts to gain her trust. I began to reinforce, I spoke to her about my feelings, I told her about work and how stressful it was to work and balance a lot of things—I began to treat her like an adult, I gave her responsibilities and toned down on the consequences, with time she began to respond to me. Then I created an interaction class, where everyone was going to share things that bothered them and we would together find a solution to the problem. By the end of the year, Karen was out of her shell and relating with people.

The point I am trying to make? All kids are not the same, there are very unique differences that each kid possesses and that uniqueness sets them apart from their peers. They all process information and experiences differently. For some if you yell, it might not have the same impact as it would have on the others. For some, you might use things they value to rope them into behaving; this method might not work, especially if you have a kid like Todd who is consistently looking for new things to love and doesn't get so attached to them like his friends would. So, evolve too. There are methods you used on them that worked when they were 1-year-old, now they are 3-years-old, would it still work?

Montessori on the other hand, designed a method of educating. This method is child centered and bases its approach on scientific processes. It has been practiced for over one hundred years in many parts of the world. The Montessori targets the child's physical, social, emotional and cognitive growth. It suggests that a child grows best in a thoughtfully prepared learning environment. In the Montessori system, the child is perceived to have a natural urge for knowledge and is capable of learning if the environment is tuned properly to initiate such a process.

These principles were developed by Maria Montessori in Rome, she opened it to teach children of low income earners who had difficulty learning. Maria noticed that pupils seemed to understand complex concepts when they engaged all their five senses. She included some activities in the school like sweeping, dusting and gardening. If they weren't doing these, they were allowed to play with the materials she designed. She also noticed that kids showed deeper concentration and repeated a particular activity.

She also realized that with time kids showed more interest in the materials she designed over other rewards like time to play with toys. She noticed that allowing kids to work independently they developed self-discipline, self-motivation and autonomy while learning. Her goal therefore was to build a system that would ensure that kids grow into independent and responsible adults that share a passion for learning and growth. The system should allow for freedom in interacting with one another, toddlers should be allowed to choose their area of learning and passion and specialized materials should be used to teach them. No grading or homework, there should be time for personal study time at least three hours a day, and mixed age classes that would allow for inter-age learning.

Montessori spoke strongly about the effect of positive discipline and positive communication on a child's growth. Positive discipline looks at mutual respect, self-sufficiency, desires. It allows the child to take control of their actions and therefore the consequence that follow. It views failure as a process or a journey that one must need to go through. It focuses on encouragement as a tool of imbibing discipline.

Positive discipline focuses on the positive character of the toddler and uses that as a tool to instill discipline. Rather than making the child's flaw very noticeable, you look at his strength and focus on that. For instance, instead of telling your child "you play too much" rather say "you can play after you do your homework", or instead of saying "Must you always ask dumb questions" you can say "Your questions are interesting, but give me some time to answer you." The idea is that you should focus on the positive side rather than elaborating the flaws of your toddler. Like we discussed earlier, kids learn more from what you do than what you say. If you want to raise positively oriented kids, you would have to reinforce the positivity.

With every flaw you notice, you want to see why the problem is there in the first place. Most times what we call flaws are just overstretched strengths. For instance, what you call stubbornness can be overstretched loyalty, what you call being overbearing, might be their ability to pay attention to details and their ability to be sensitive to other people's feelings. What you might call talking too much, might be a person just trying to express themselves. You would always find strength in weakness and you should focus more on the strength than building castles on the negative outcome. You should also learn to reinforce the behavior you want to see, rather than speaking about the behavior you do not want to see.

To properly engage positive discipline, you must learn good communication and conflict resolution. Some parents don't believe in communicating with their kids. They impose whatever they want to impose on the kids hoping the kid would bend the knee and do what they want. They might get away with it while the kid is still a toddler, but when the child matures and believes he can bear the consequence of defying you, he/she would. Why? They have learnt the limit to your threats and now they can call your bluff. Positive discipline affects you the trainer and the parent, you can now contain your emotions and think objectively.

But there is a side to this we ought to pay attention to; Maria Montessori said, "To let a child do as he likes, when he has not yet developed any powers of control, it so to betray the idea of freedom."

If you notice that your children have not understood delayed gratification and some other basic disciplines, you cannot give them autonomy yet. Free will if explored without inner discipline, you would create a monster instead of a responsible adult. Parents/trainers/teachers are just guides, your job is to monitor the progress of your toddler, look at areas where the toddler is still groping and needs help, then guide him through the process, but do not interfere with the process, just guide.

Montessori looks more at utilizing the child's own ability to build self-discipline. It is easier to get someone to do something they believe is the best for them, if your toddler can recognize that this activity is beneficial to him/her they would by themselves begin to engage in the act without you even being there to guide them.

You'd notice at a point in your child's growth, he/she would not like you to feed them anymore, or give them a bath; they want to show you that they can do it too. If you encourage that attitude, they would eventually learn to carry the activity without your supervision. Do not interfere, if a child believes he/she can do something, don't interfere, let them carry on, they would eventually catch up.

Positive discipline PRESERVES the child's dignity and esteem. Anything that would make the child struggle with his esteem is not healthy in any way to the kid. You want to be sure that as you discipline them, their esteem is intact and they are going to evolve based on a healthy self-esteem and correct view about failure. Don't belittle your toddlers; don't cause them to view you negatively. If you make a mistake, be quick to apologize and explain to them how wrong what you did was; they would learn quickly not to indulge in any behavior that shreds their esteem.

When your child does something wrong you want to be sure if that in itself is wrong or if you are just exhausted.

You really want to pause to think if the action was done out of curiosity or it was a direct flaunting of your instructions. When you can figure out which it is, you would know what to do next. Dialogue is a very good way to getting your children to see that they have overstepped the line. They can think too!

Most times, the only thing we know about discipline is the one our parents did to us and more often than not it doesn't always work well with our kids. Dialogue with them, ask them why they did what they did, if they realize they did something wrong they would show remorse, if they did something wrong and aren't remorseful, you have to explain to them that what they did was wrong. I remember a parent saying to me that she had a problem with her kid who turned on the gas cooker, and began putting paper inside. The smoke alarm went off and alerted her. She ran into the kitchen and saw what he did; she said the kid knew he did something wrong and was only remorseful for few minutes. She said she expected him to be remorseful for maybe the whole day and sit still!

I am sure we all want those energetic kids to sit still after they do some damage; the truth is the kid would recover from guilt because he felt loved, he didn't feel condemned even by his action. I told her that it was a good thing for him at this stage. A time in his growth would come when if he does something really terrible he would understand the gravity of it and by then he might also have learnt to have a healthy self-esteem and responsibility. Even then, he should not be afraid of you or what you would do; he should just feel disappointed because he hurt someone who loves him.

If your child's reaction to you correcting him is powered by love, you would never lose that child's trust. He/she would be comfortable with you and see reasons quickly why they need to correct whatever damage they are doing—they need to understand that it's not okay to hurt anyone. These are things your kids would learn as a result of dialogue.

If you want to discipline a child positively, avoid using fear as a tool. It is more damaging than it is helpful; rather than fear, use love, let them not view correction as something someone who hates them does, let them see correction as love—if they can see this clearly, you can easily correct them and it would have a tremendous impact on their growth.

HISTORICAL INTRODUCTION TO THE MONTESSORI DISCIPLINE

The Montessori educational discipline is a modern method of teaching that was being created by Maria Montessori. It is a child-centered educational method of teaching in which children are allowed to make use of their psychological instincts to learn in a comfortable environment and at their own pace.

In Montessori, teachers view the students (children) and the classroom as a different entity, it focuses on harnessing the true potential in a child by respecting the individualistic differences in the children. This means that Montessori education believes that all children are different and then finds a way of harnessing these individualistic strengths. This is done by encouraging these strengths and providing an enabling environment to help nurture the strengths of the children and also promoting the social, emotional and physical interaction among the students.

Features of a Montessori discipline

- In the Montessori academic discipline, children of mixed age range are classified in a class e.g 0 -3, 3-6, 6-9, 9-12, 12-15, 15-18 years old are classed in accordance with the range.

- The children are given enough time to work, uninterrupted by either teachers or any other factors within the environment. The reason for this is so that children can find out their imaginative skills and also foster relationships among the children. This relationship can generate a problem-solving character in them, also it increases their social well-being.

- It also brings about discovery. As students are left alone, it results in them discovering things on their own without direct inputs from teachers. Getting answers to the questions on their own, finding a solution to the problem they've observed.

- Students are given the liberty to choose their own preferred activities from various available options.

- Availability of an environment which allows students to work freely and have access to available materials needed for learning and quick assimilation.

- The liberty of the student must be placed under the prescribed limits of the class.

- Teachers are meant to observe and note the development of each student. Also, teachers can contribute to the students' work, just that the contribution is limited and not full thorough participation. The teacher observes the abilities of each student, resilience to a task, skills of the student and the child's intrinsic characters.

The Montessori educational discipline classroom is beautifully ordered to create the best impression for quick learning and assimilation in students at their different age range.

Maria believes that the classroom is necessary for building a child's reasonability and that it must be prepared to meet the needs of the student at their specific age range.

She opined that when students learn on their own it creates a form of experience for them and this will, in turn, help them to be better in any activities or subjects they engage in. Social integration has an important role to play in students' productivity in that everyone will see themselves as not independent but dependent on others to fulfill their aims.

The classroom comprises materials that will help the development of the students, creating a match between the curiosity of the student and the materials available in the classroom.

HISTORY OF MONTESSORI EDUCATIONAL DISCIPLINE

Dr. Maria Montessori is a physician, an educator and a scientist who has a passion for how to better understand the best student in the classroom as opposed to the traditional teacher to student classroom settings.

She was invited by a couple to establish a home for the children (a childcare home) where her psychological experiment can be put into practice. In this childcare, she worked with the less privileged children and also with children who are not opportune to go to school due to their impoverished states.

People labeled this kind of children very slow to learn and that their ability to understand in school is limited but Dr. Maria was ready to prove otherwise.

On January 6, 1907, Casa Dei Bambini (which is interpreted as children's house) was opened by Dr. Maria and she was willing to make Casa Dei Bambini an educationally safe haven for this children, through the provision of a serene environment and other necessary materials for easy learning and character cultivation for the kids.

Dr. Maria saw that these students were at first showing unwillingness to learn but as time went by they started showing a positive attitude towards learning.

One distinctive feature of these students was their readiness, willingness and drive to be taught by the environment and everyone's knowledge gotten by them was auto-didactic (self-taught). They later showed interest in solving difficult puzzles, taking care of the environment and making their meals themselves. She also observed that children normally carry out deep concentration when things are new to them, and then practice them on their own, this creates learning experiences in them.

Dr. Maria formulated a design for learning and also came up with unusual learning materials and equipment that help facilitate easy and comprehensive learning for the students. She also created an enabling environment that she thought will improve the natural desire of children to learn.

These designs for learning were gotten from her years of scientific observation and expertise she gained from her previous works with the young children.

THE RISE OF MONTESSORI EDUCATION

Dr. Maria's Montessori accomplishments in Italy began to draw attention all around the world. People started viewing education differently from the normal conventional methods of education. In no time, inquisitors, who are passionate about learning this new technique started trouping into Italy to have a first-hand experience of the Montessori education and to see for themselves the children transformed by it. Many concluded that Montessori is the best educational approach because it focuses on self-discipline and concentration as demonstrated by the students at Casa Dei Bambini.

Dr. Maria started teaching people (educators) from different parts of the world the Montessorian education approach, she drew out courses and taught them to many who were willing to learn.

Within a few years of existence, the Montessori approach had already spread across some continents of the world.

Dr. Maria's first book titled the Montessori methods (Il Metodo della Pedagogia Scientifica applicate all'educazione infantile nelle Case Dei bambini) was published in 1909. Within some years the book had been translated into 10 languages. The English version of the book sold out 5000 copies in just four days.

The Montessori school grew much in western Europe and around the world by 1910 and by 1911 the first Montessorian school was established in the United States of America (USA).

Praises started trouping in for Dr. Maria Montessori and the Montessori approach from educational scholars and different magazines worldwide.

In 1917, Dr. Maria published another book which narrates her stance on the education of children within the age range of 7-11. She titled the book L'autoeducazionne nelle Scuole Elementary (the translation in English is The Advanced Montessori Method.)

Maria Montessori's new Montessori research

In the early years of Montessori development, it focuses on the education of young children between the early stages of their development. But by the 1920s, Dr. Maria shifted her focus into a more complex age, the age of adolescence.

She opined that children in this category need to find their purpose, engage in activities that will help them to figure out who they really are, help them discover their position in the world and how to figure out procedures to help them be a responsible human being to the society as a whole.

At that time, she recommended schools (that is residential in nature) where young adolescents can live in, study and be productive. Here, she believed that the school will be in the form of a community where the young adolescents can work in, live in and form relationships that are trustworthy. She opined that these adolescents can engage in entrepreneurial activities like making handmade goods and marketing these products themselves.

Her reason for including entrepreneurial skills and marketing is to help them learn interdependence and how to best meet the needs of society at large.

In 1929, Dr. Maria and her son Mario established the first Montessori association called the Association of Montessori International so as to guarantee that the rudiments of the approach and the ideology behind the Montessori education are preserved and carried on as planned by her.

Montessori educational movement in America

In 1911 the first Montessori school was opened in the United States of America. It was established in the home of a prominent banker in Scarborough, New York City. As soon as it was opened, the success in America led to several other Montessori schools in the United States.

It's believed that the Montessori school in America was established for kids from rich backgrounds, cultured households who are trying to give their kids the best education.

Dr. Maria Montessori traveled to America in 1913, her reason was to teach and make the Montessori approach more prominent in America. She performed a 3-week lecture tour for the curious educators and interested crowd.

In Washington, D.C. it was believed that Dr. Maria lectured more than 400 willing audiences including some prominent people.

Also, a lecture was arranged for her at New York City's Carnegie Hall, where she lectured an audience of up to 1000 people using moving pictures that were taken in her school (Cara Pei Mbini).

After her successful trip to the United States of America, she went back home but returned to America in 1915 to help train and give courses to teachers who were willing to adopt the Montessori techniques.

While she was in America she pioneered the building of a glass Montessori classroom. She said this structure will still help educators observe the progress of the students in the class. The major thing to observe about them is the students' concentration, focus, and priority on the tasks given to them.

In 1915, the National Education Association in Oakland, California had its conference in which Dr. Maria was invited as a guest speaker. It was recorded that more than 15,000 educators were present for the conference.

More Montessori schools were established by 1916 and the success of the Montessori glass classroom led to the adoption and creation of the Montessori education in the United States.

William Kilpatrick's criticism of Montessori education.

The rise of Montessori education in America was not without criticism. William Kilpatrick, a former student of the American psychologist and education reformer John Dewey critiqued the Montessori method of education.

Kirkpatrick criticized the Montessori approach in his book, The Montessori System Examined. He rejected the Montessori approach of the limited role of the teacher, the modality of the classroom and also the freedom given to the students.

This criticism and negative appraisal were spread all over the United States of America and then caused a decline in the adoption and practice of the Montessori approach and by 1920s the Montessori education approach had almost vanished.

The Rebirth of Montessori in the United States of America

An aspiring teacher Nancy McCormick Rambusch stumbled on Dr. Maria Montessori's writings on the Montessori approach to education, she was fascinated by her approach and felt it was more scientific and systematic.

During the 1950s the conventional education approaches had started to fail and people were feeling dissatisfied with it. This made Nancy look for answers to conventional education approaches.

She attended a Montessori Congress in Paris to learn more about it and there she met Mario Montessori (Dr. Maria's son) and they spoke about reintroducing the Montessori education approach back to America.

Through rigorous study and extensive consultation, Nancy reintroduced the approach in the United States and started the American Montessori Society in 1960.

What Montessori education tends to achieve.

Every parent wants the best for their kids and they will be willing to give anything for the proper upbringing of their children.

The Montessori education cares about learning aimed at bringing the best out of children, making them see the strength in themselves and how they can channel this strength towards solving a purported or perceived problem.

Parents will be willing to enroll their children where they can develop to be problem-solving adults, building their interpersonal skills and create a sense of responsibility. These are the core values Montessori tends to accomplish, these values are directed to improving the social, emotional and cognitive strength of the students.

The following are the values Montessori education tends to achieve

- Knowledge: Montessori education focuses on nurturing students and building concentration and self-confidence for them. This, in turn, will help the student put more effort to gain more knowledge in their endeavors. The classroom is equipped with the necessary materials and facilities required to help them gain more knowledge. The approach enables one to easily flow with the lessons and give the capacity to enlighten oneself and to think about what one is learning over time.

- Fosters resourceful relationships: Montessori education allows the students to relate with each other and solve problems together. Through this relationship, cooperation and trust are built among the students. This cooperation will increase the rate at which problems are easily solved because brainstorming is encouraged. As students grow up they feel the sense of belonging to a much larger community and that they have a duty to perform in the outside world. This, however, doesn't disturb the students from choosing their own paths and learning in line with it.

- Increases student capacity: The Montessorian classroom is designed to help students increase their imaginative strengths. The necessary apparatus needed for this is provided in the class; students have no restrictions whatsoever working with these apparatuses to help them fully understand what they are capable of doing. Also, in the Montessorian classroom, children are given the liberty to choose their activities out of available options and work in line with these activities without any obstruction. Allowing students to choose their activities does not affect them negatively but it creates an innate motivation and sets a very solid foundation for the development of the students.

- Accountability: The Montessorian classroom is created in such a way that students have the liberty to learn in there with little or no contribution from the teacher. They have their space, necessary materials for them to work with, and reasonable time for them to finish their tasks. These tasks are not fully directed by the teachers, but the students. This means that students are accountable for their works. However, teachers are charged with the responsibility of observing and recording the daily observed interaction of the students with their peers and the environment, coming up with a plan to help them become better, but not doing the work for them, or are not directly involved with the class exercises. The student's unique interest will help the teachers to know how best to nurture and facilitate the former's skills. The Montessorian classroom approach helps students to assess and correct themselves where needed. Though self-correction may not be easy during the early years of a child, as they mature they begin to assess themselves more intimately and correct themselves where necessary.

MONTESSORI METHODS

If you are new to Montessori education, you may be forced to ask what makes Montessori different from every other form of education. Predominantly, there are many methods of teaching, each aiming at helping kids grow and develop but none of them is child and level oriented like Montessori.

Of course, every parent is concerned about finding the best educational program for their children. We all recognize the lasting impact that early learning experiences have on a child's growth, development and future learning. The best way to sum this up is that Montessori education is not just a qualitative and better approach to preparing a child, it is a thriving and conducive method of education that allows your child to grow at their own pace and learn with all needed efficiency.

Several elements of the Montessori approach meet the required educational goals which today's parents have for their children, which includes children who are conscious of themselves and grow into capable people and have the potential to be productive throughout their lives.

With Montessori education, the growth starts early. The best years to set the foundation of who a child will become is the early years (from birth through to age six). This is the time to set the platform of who the child will become and the role to play in the future. Montessori education is therefore aimed at developing kids who are capable, accountable, knowledgeable and self-conscious

The Montessori method is characterized by providing and preparing a ready environment that is tidy, conducive and pleasing in appearance where every element exists to aid the development of the child. The classroom is designed to integrate children of mixed ages that are grouped in periods of 3 years. This helps the kids socialize with kids of their age. It breeds respect for their peers among them. It solidifies solidarity among them naturally.

The environment offers the child lots of opportunities to commit to interesting and freely chosen work, this makes the children become more concentrated as there are enough gadgets and equipment to keep them busy. Freedom develops within clear limits and this makes the children live in peace and tranquility with others in their classroom, therefore creating a harmonious society.

There are concrete materials that children work with, this provides them the viable keys to explore the world and develop basic cognitive abilities. These materials help the kids to be able to identify their own errors, how to correct mistakes or re-make decisions and become responsible for their own learning.

This won't be done without the supervision of adults. The adult is an observer and a guide. They help to stimulate and direct the child with their effort. This helps the children to act, want, think and direct by themselves. It fosters and develops their confidence and inner discipline. Instead of instructing with prepared lectures, handouts, worksheets and lesson plans as found in traditional teaching, a Montessori teacher will offer guidance but the child is in charge of his or her own learning. The most important and greatest achievement of Montessori education is that it allows for children to work, learn and develop at their own individual pace. Their skillset is highlighted and hyped so that they can progress in their development as an individual.

The sequence of Montessori lessons aligns well, and in many cases exceeds, state learning standards, ensuring that children are made to go through complex learning concepts through hands-on experiences that enhance deeper and full understanding.

Montessori education is an all-compassing method, as it covers all periods of learning and education from birth to age 18, therefore providing an integrated and developing curriculum for them all.

The drive behind Montessori education is the philosophy of creating and encouraging a love for learning. Montessori children remain curious about the people and the world around them. They see learning as an enjoyable life-long process rather than a burden that is lifted up as soon as the school bell is rung. This benefit can make a child so much committed to learning their entire lives and become a propelling force through secondary education, career, job training or experiences they have and develop.

The Montessori Environment

Montessori environments are prepared in advance based on observations of the students' individual abilities. The environment is a spacious, open, tidy, pleasing in appearance, a simple and real place, where each element is placed for strategic reasons, in order to help the development of the child.

The environment of each classroom is descriptive of the height and size of the children the class is meant for. Each class has low shelves, tables, and chairs of different sizes where children can sit individually or in groups.

The classroom is specifically themed and targeted. It is to show theme areas where related materials and equipment are exposed on the shelves. The classroom often contains several stations, each containing toys that allow children to explore while learning. It is very common to see a station in a Montessori classroom have a bucket of Lego blocks and several pictures of simple objects like an apple or a house, which can heighten the sense of the children to try building structures if they want. Each child uses the materials he chooses by taking it from the shelf and returning it in its place so others can make use of it.

The environment is made to promote the child's interdependence in exploring and learning. The idea behind the Montessori classroom is allowing children to learn through playing. Freedom and self-discipline make it possible that each child finds activities that are in connection to their needs and conscious development.

Montessori classrooms gather children in 3 classes of age; those younger than 3 years old, those who are between age 3 to age 6, those from age 6 to age 9 and from 9 to 13 years old. These mixed-age classrooms foster spontaneous cooperation and desire to learn. It aids mutual respect and the acquisition of deep knowledge while teaching others. Notably, the reason for mixed-age grouping is for younger children to watch older children play. This process is referred to as scaffolding and it is a method of social learning populated by Le Vygotsky.

The growth of the child

The aim of the Montessori method is that every educator should 'follow the child' to recognize their growth (evolutionary needs) and the characteristics of their age. With the understanding of their needs comes a need to build a favorable environment (physical and spiritual) to respond to these needs. The development of children emerges as a need to adapt to his/her environment. Children need to give meaning to the world that surrounds them by how they construct themselves in relation to this world.

Maria Montessori noted that the child goes through four ambivalent evolutionary periods called 'Planes of Development'. Each period reveals characteristics that are seriously different from the other periods. However, each period is a foundation for the next period and what to expect.

The first plane of development according to Maria Montessori starts at birth and continues until the child is 6 years old. She noticed that this period is characterized by children's "Absorbent Mind" which takes and absorbs everything whether good or bad from the environment that surrounds him or her. The child even picks up the language and culture of their primary environment through this method. In the second plane, from age 6 to age 12, the child possesses a "rational mind" to amaze the world with their imagination, abstract thinking, and creativity. The 'third plane' is marked from age 12 to age 18, the teenager develops a "humanistic mind" which seeks to understand humanity and contribute to society. The last plane of development is from age 18 to 24 years old, the adult explores the world from a "specialist mind" where he tries to find his or her place in the world.

Materials

Montessori materials are scientifically designed to pay special attention to a child's interest based on the evolutionary stage he is going through and with the belief that manipulating concrete objects increases the development of knowledge and aids abstract thinking.

Montessori materials are made in a way to allow children to investigate and explore things in a personal and independent way. Their continuous repetition and concentration promotes creativity. They, therefore, develop abilities to isolate difficulties, as each material introduces a special and unique variable. It makes the children develop newer concepts, leaving older concepts or modifying them.

Materials here have a control of error. This means that with time, the continuous use of these materials will show the child if he/she used them correctly. This way, children will know what errors they have committed and later understand that errors are part of the learning process. This imbibes positive attitudes into children as it makes them responsible for their own learning and developing their self-confidence.

The Montessori Teacher

The Montessori method nurtures order, concentration, coordination and independence. by having specialized teachers often called "directress" observe each child. They equally observe his needs, capabilities and interests, growth and development and offer him or her the opportunity to work intelligently with a concrete purpose, and to service the care of the child in the classroom. The major objective of the teacher is to allow the child to grow by offering reduced intervention through self-development. The child is allowed to act, want and think for himself/herself, thus helping him or her to develop confidence and inner discipline. There is basically no award of praise or apportioning of blames as this might distort the inner balance of another child, instead of each child finding inner satisfaction that comes from the success of their personal works.

In a Montessori classroom, teachers assess students on a daily basis, using the observations of each class in the environment and among peers as a record keeper. They use the development and academic performance of each child to prepare an environment that is stimulating academically, rewarding physically, encompassing socially and developing emotionally. This develops an individualized learning plan for each child, based on his or her unique interests and abilities. The teachers abound to provide environments where students have the freedom and the tools to seek answers to their inquisitiveness and seek out new knowledge themselves.

Should there be a need for an introduction of new materials because the child is ready for new lessons, the directress will note this based on the evolutionary development of the child and present activities individually or in a group. The teacher is not responsible for the learning of the child, instead, it is the child who is responsible for his or her own learning and development.

The Curriculum

The beginning of a child's future is altruistically set during his or her first three years of life. Montessori named this period, the "spiritual embryo", in which the child does in the psychological sphere. This is achieved through the child's absorbent mind (the first plane of development) which integrates experiences, relations, emotions, languages, and culture through his or her sense. The life experiences the child has shapes his or her senses and brains, forming networks that have the potential of staying with the person for all of his or her life.

From birth to 3 years old, the Montessori education aims at the development of their speaking, coordinated movements, and independence, which is to give the child inbuilt confidence and allows him or her to discover his or her potential and his or her place within the community.

From age 3 to 6 years

- Practical life: activities aimed at the care of the person, of others and of the physical environment where they live. Activities like washing, polishing, setting the table, arranging flowers, etc.

- Sensorial: children learn through their senses at this age. Materials they interact with and use here are made to refine each of their senses. Each is to indicate and recognize a specific quality, smell, size, weight, texture, flavor, and color, etc.

- Language: children build their language bank at this age. They learn to write, starting with their senses (hearing and touching), and learn to read. Children know about geography, history, arts, and music. These areas help children to know about their surroundings and understand the place they occupy in this world.

- Math: materials help the child to learn and understand mathematical concepts as these materials egg them to develop their intuitiveness to abstract concepts; like algebra and geometry.

From age 6 to 12

The classroom curriculum for children from 6 to age 12 presents an evolutionary, historical, integrated and complete vision of knowledge and human development. There are five important and great lessons, otherwise known as fundamental lessons from which specific studies of different areas will develop. The lessons here, are designed to arouse and awaken the imagination, curiosity, and admiration for the creative and unimaginable innovative capacity of the unshackled human spirit.

Here, children are made to learn Astronomy, Meteorology, chemistry, physics, geography to know and understand the origin of the universe and the Earth. They undergo lessons of the 'coming of life' through Biology, Botany, Environment, Evolution of life, Zoology. History, Culture, Social studies, scientific discoveries, and inventions help to learn of the 'coming of Human Being'. Reading, writing, language structures, literature, and linguistics teach Communication. They learn numbers and figuration through Math, the origin of numbers, systems of numbers, trigonometry and geometry.

Differences between the Montessori Method and the Traditional Teaching Method

- Montessori lessons are hands-on and active. Students are encouraged to discover their passions themselves through materials. Students are made to memorize, cram, and take tests in the Traditional Method of teaching.
- Students are granted as much time as needed to work on lessons, interruptions are minimal and reduced. Time limitations are mandated in traditional classrooms, they work on a fixed terminal schedule and must make sure they cover the syllabus within that time frame.
- Montessori curricula expand and reduce in response to the needs of the students. Traditional curricula are

predetermined without looking out for the child, it is fixed and rigid.

- Montessori curricula are aimed at appealing to the child's innate hunger for knowledge. Children learn to love learning. Traditional curricula have a standard test performance and grade which children must learn because it is mandatory.

- Grade levels in Montessori schools are flexible and determined by the developmental range of the child (i.e 0-3, 3-6, 6-9, 9-12, 12-15 years of age). In traditional schools, grade levels are rigid and strictly defined by age within a twelve-month period.

- Children in Montessori curricula develop self-esteem through their accomplishments and an internal sense of pride. The traditional method of teaching gives validation through external judgment and assessment.

ADVICE FOR NEW VULNERABLE MOTHERS

WHO IS A VULNERABLE MOTHER?

Firstly, before we proceed to give advice to mothers about tips to effective communication with their kids, there is a need to understand who the vulnerable mothers are in the context of child communication. Vulnerable mothers are those mothers who are susceptible to a child's miscommunication.

These mothers may have in one way or the other ineffective procedures or ways by which their idea is communicated to their kids and when this idea is communicated, the kids tend to neglect their importance, or they do not see the need to obey the instruction because they, as kids cannot decode the content of the information or instruction, passed across.

The place of a mother in her children's upbringing can never be belittled. This is owing to the fact that mothers leave a lasting imprint or influence on the life of their young ones through their relationship and this imprint can make or mar the child's developmental etiquette.

The mind structure of kids is soft but reflective. A kid's mind has the capacity to receive a piece of information passed across to it, then it ponders on it to reflect a meaningful comprehension and when the comprehension is attained, it is then we can say a child has the ability to give feedback or response to the information earlier sent. But if the manner of process at which the information is passed is not equivalent to the reflective capacity of the child, then he tends to go delinquent and disregard any information more complex than his mind.

Therefore, mothers who have a problem communicating either an idea or an instruction to the kid are often referred to as vulnerable mothers in this regard.

For example, some years ago, while I was in my office, a woman in her early thirties walked into my office and told me how the communication between her and her 5-year-old child has degenerated. In my discourse with her, I understood that she enforces her decision on her child; she doesn't care to hear about the opinion of the child. In her opinion, the child is too little to dictate her view; she believed she's mentally immature for it.

Mothers who do not want to hear their kid's opinion are very susceptible to miscommunication with them. When this happens, kids become extremely intolerant. Kids can be small yet they have a reasoning ability which must not be undermined, they have a voice that needs to be listened to and the inability of mothers to be patient enough to hear views gives them a license to endanger their communicative relationship with their kids.

Mothers must be very careful in the way of dealing with their kids. Most kids have the capacity to study the status quo of their relationship with their parents and develop a mindset around this. In the formative years of their development they tend to study the situation around the family, retain most information as they come and then try to adopt that information they have stored up over the years. When this happens, they develop a school of thought around the things they have learnt in their formative years.

Mothers should be very wary of this, it is in these years that the mother needs to be very attentive and lay a very moral foundation for the kids, and this can only be done through communication morals in the right manner and at the right time. Inability to do this may result in an adoption of an improper culture which may be injurious to his society.

I must also verify that there are no universally accepted approaches that can serve as a trusty compass to an effective child-parent relationship as the character of every child is distinct and also that of the parent.

Therefore, every mother must know how to better understand her kids and build a relationship around these understanding. This will go a long way in improving the transmission of any vital information from the parent to the kids without any shortcoming.

EXAMPLES OF NEW VULNERABLE MOTHERS

In my years of practice, I've seen different factors that have contributed to the reasons why mothers are vulnerable to having difficulty in communicating morals to kids.

This made me draw out examples of mothers who are likely to be vulnerable to impacting the lesson of disciplines and morals to their children. It must be noted that one cannot force a kid to do what he or she does not want to see, if these sets of disciplinary measures are forced in children, they tend to form rigid developmental walls against them and then evolve to become obstinate against those measures.

Therefore, below are clearly outlined examples of mothers who are most likely to be vulnerable:

1. Single Mothers: these are women who don't have a husband but live with their child (ren). Such may have a full or partial custody of the children. Single mothers are always responsible for the upkeep of their children, they are pretty much occupied, and this occupation may lead to pressure on them. This pressure may, in turn, give them a lack of time for their children. They are most under pressure to make sure that their children are well catered for and politely groomed in all areas. This pressure, however positive, rids them of their time of communication with their kids. They are more often than not in a hurry over everything and have probably no time to listen to the little details from their children. I met a single mother some years ago, who came to see me about how inattentive her 6 years-old boy had become, I asked her when she last sought for her son's opinion, I asked her when she last went on a vacation with him. Her reply was since he was 4. She went on to narrate how uneasy it was taking care of him, how busy she has

become over the years trying to take care of her baby. Instantly I knew the weak chain in the relationship between the mother and the child. As good as it is, catering to the needs of the kids must never be done at the detriment of the connection that exists between the mother and the child. Single mothers need to learn how to bridge the gap between caring for the needs of their children and having time for them. They are two different things, while one is taking care of them materially; the other is giving the children credibility to trust their parent. This will help mothers a lot to better understand the situation and better improve their relationship with their children.

2. Disabled mothers: disabled mothers are those mothers that have mental or physical disabilities and are also charged with the responsibility of raising and taking care of their kids. Mothers with disabilities are saddled with the responsibility of also bringing up their children morally, academically and socially but just that they do not

have full abilities as the able mother. Disabled Mothers are always charged with the problem of communicating effectively with their children, they would always want to raise their children in the right way but may not have the abilities to channel instructions properly to their lads. Children tend to take this as an opportunity to exploit their mother's weakness by not listening to the prescribed piece of communication sent to them. A parent sent me a mail on how to better understand their third child because he's never ready to listen to his mother who has a disability. After reading the mail she sent to me, I observed that the child will always bank on the disability of the mother not to listen to her because he felt his opinion should always matter. I returned the mail by giving them necessary steps to follow and also explicitly indicated that the husband has a role to play in this case. When a mother is disabled one of the best ways to curtail a child's behavior is that the husband must be very available to help communicate the best idea to the child. He must be the strength of the woman; he must be willing to help her instill discipline on the lads. Knowing how vulnerable his wife is at that moment, he must be able to stand in and fill the gap for the woman, as they are meant to be each other's support after all. It is necessary to know that children who have very good communication with their disabled mothers tend to develop into emotionally balanced individuals, more passionate and loving, and ever ready to help. This is as a result of the prior understanding of their mother's plight and readiness to adapt. Therefore, raising a kid by a disabled mother requires joint participation of both the mother and the father to carefully design ways of communicating ideas, morals and values properly without obstruction to their kids.

3. Busy mothers: these are mothers who are always occupied with a task or job, either for the family or for personal attainment (career-wise). Time is always an important factor in communication, a

piece of information must be passed across at the right time, if the timing is wrong, then it will reduce the potency of the result it is intended to achieve. An example of this is giving active instructions to kids when they are stressed, stress at that particular time invalidates the potency of the information. Stress will reduce the active senses required to listen and produce an instant response. Though the information came through the right channel, the timing was wrong. Busy mothers are sometimes not attentive because they do not have all the time in the world to listen, this can serve as an impediment to the development of the child because children must be given adequate attention and vigilance in their early stage of development. It is this attention and vigilance that will help guide them to the next phase of their development ladder. Busy mothers are vulnerable to hampering the moral and ethical development of their kids. As it is necessary to take care of the children, it is also mandatory to have time for them, listen to them, study them and nurture them right. This way, children will grow up fully equipped for life's challenges thrown at them. What a child will become tomorrow is a consequence of the quality of his/her nurturing today.

4. Autocratic mothers: this can also be referred to as authoritarian mothers. This kind of mothers believes the kids should not be heard, they believe a kid's responses are irrelevant as long as they do not correspond with their own perspective and view about a matter. When it comes to setting standards, they would rather set the rules and standards for the kids not minding the input of the children. They plan for them without their consent; they never take the beliefs of the children into account because they believe it doesn't matter. This type of mothers are very vulnerable because they destroy the kid's self-confidence and enthusiasm. Because autocratic mothers take decisions for their kids, the latter grow up to be indecisive about their true self when it comes to facing their own

mountain, they turn out to be over-reliant. Children who grow up with autocratic mothers tend to become more aggressive and hostile. Such kids harbor a feeling of anger and resentment toward their parents because their mothers focus more on punishment. To avoid punishment, such kids may develop overtime the ability to lie. They are so much entrenched in fear making them unable to reveal their (children) heart to their mothers. Many years ago, I had neighbors who nag over almost everything, this one was too picky over little things and this made her little children uncomfortable being around her. She will raise her voice at them at will and question the children's decisions over their engagement. At a long, she started losing their trust, they could not confide in her, they preferred to talk to me, share with me their problems. I gave them the liberty to truly express themselves and through that I started communicating morals into them. Their mother wants them to be responsible but she has a problem communicating that idea to them, she wants them to do things her way disregarding their feelings. Later on, her children started isolating themselves from her, they don't want to talk to her, they don't want to be around her. She eventually came to me and I explained to her how she's been too rigid in her approach of trying to communicate.

ADVICE FOR NEW VULNERABLE MOTHERS

Having carefully spelled out who the vulnerable mothers are there's need to give advice on how to have effective communication with children in order to bring out the best in them either mentally, emotionally, academically or socially. This set of advice will help the mother have a relationship with their children.

1. Study your children: it's essential for mothers to understand the personality of their children. A child's personality varies from one child to another.

The mother must be aware of this fact and consciously develop their technique towards the personality of each child. SWOT (strength, weakness, opportunity and threat) Analysis may be adapted to know the personality of a child. Mothers must be able to determine the strength and weakness of their children and take a very realistic approach to it and also know what the child's definition of opportunity and threat as pertaining to himself is. By doing this, mothers will build conscious developmental and communication techniques around it.

2. Allocate time for your children: this is a very crucial element in character building and development in children. The mother must understand that she doesn’t just have to tender to the physical needs of the children but also to bear psychological, moral, and social needs. Time must be allocated to children so you can be closer to them. Children need to be loved, catered for, and to do this it takes time. As you spend time with

your kids as a mother, some of their personality begins to open to you, and through that make the right decision that will improve the development of your kids.

3. Share your life experiences with your children: most mothers keep their last life away from their children. One of the best ways of communicating with your kids is to share your past experiences with them. Tell them what you did right and where you made a mistake, this will serve as guidelines for them in the various stages of their development. Remember you also have passed through that stage, so when you share your life's experiences with them, it makes them aware of a possible opportunity or threat as they go on in life.

4. Have listening ears: mothers should learn to be attentive to their children, this is key to getting hold of the important happenings in your children's life. While growing up my mom was my best friend, I told her everything going on in my life,

she was so attentive and ready to listen, she didn't try to live my life for me but her advice shaped most of my decisions in my teenage years. Children love the company of listening mothers and they will be ready to pour out their mind to them (mothers).

5. Never enforce opinions on them: children love it when they do things their way, learn to advise them and don't force your way into their minds. A mother who does this will make the children reluctant to relay their thoughts to her. Mothers should learn to use the best method that suits the personality of the children to communicate with them.

BUILDING CONFIDENCE IN MOTHERS

As earlier stated, a mother plays a significant role in child development. To be good in this role is to be confident in attaining success in it.

Firstly, consistency is a trait that mothers need to adopt, it is good to start the necessary techniques towards raising a responsible human in a child but being consistent is better. Mothers need to find delight in trying to help their kids grow up being a better person fulfilling their greatest potentials to the fullest from time to time. Kids can be disturbing but you need to find your place around them confidently.

Accessing the weakness of the child isn't an easy task, it takes much conscious effort and also takes time. That is why mothers must be steady with these developmental steps and have keen passion for trying to bring out the best in them.

Morals and societal values are the core values of human existence and they are instilled right from the early stages of a child's development.

Mothers have a very cordial relationship with their children in their early stage of development, that's why they must be willing to enter into this stage with them (kids) fully committed and dedicated to the task, ever listening to them, devoting time and resources. These are not easy but as a mother, you have to enter into it with much confidence and enthusiasm.

Trust is a very important way to build confidence, many mothers feel insecure about their kids, probably because of a perceived inadequacy that may present itself, or because they lack the strength to stay ever conscious to the needs of their kids.

As a mother, you must learn to trust your kids as this gives you confidence in helping them be better humans. The ease of the job is as a result of the confidence you have garnered to help develop your child.

Children are very good learners, they learn pretty fast and they are very observant about their environment, they notice the events happening around them, study the situation and adopt that which has more influence on them. That's why a mother must be positively influential in these formative years of the child's development stage. She must be adept in employing the right methods that will boost her relationship with the kids.

Fear and discouragement may pose as a threat to this confidence which the mother has garnered, the fear of raising the kids wrongly; the fear of not putting much effort can also dent the confidence of a mother in relating with her children.

At every stage of development, challenges will always surface, and the inability of a child to move past the challenge that presented itself in the phases of development will stop him from progressing into the next stage of development.

Therefore, mothers must understand the task at hand, do it with confidence and perseverance so as to help their kids overcome the challenges in each stage.

The family is the first means of learning for little kids; they develop their ideology from their parents or anyone in the house, before a child learns from the society he first learns from the family, therefore, the basis of what he's to learn outside the family is pressured on what he learnt in the family.

BUILDING CONFIDENCE IN KIDS

As kids grow up, there is a need for them to believe in themselves and build confidence, find their comforts or discomforts. This character is needed for proper development of every child. The foundation of confidence is laid right in the formative years of their phases of development.

Confidence is having a certainty of what one is capable of doing, to be firm in decision-making, and having self-assurance in circumstances that would necessarily bring fear. The psychological pattern of a child must be directed towards the attainment of certain goals, and to achieve this goal, they must be confident that they can do it.

Living their day to day life, children too can experience certain difficulty, this is why it is up to parents to build a sufficient level of confidence not just for them to exist or survive but to withstand any threats and thrive in any situations.

What makes confident children is their ability to be practical, logical and optimistic about their abilities and the perception they have towards problem-solving situations.

Parents should learn to motivate their children with sweet words and praise whenever they make good use of their abilities, by so doing their confidence is built to do better next time.

Confidence makes children believe in themselves. As we know children will always try new things, when they fail at something, it's a lesson for them to try again harder in a different way in order to succeed, and to work even harder to surpass their previous achievement. As elementary as this task may be, it serves as a step onto a bigger challenge in the next phase of development.

Confidence starts from the child's early stage, they build confidence through being loved, cared and catered for, and being accepted. As the baby grows, he/she carries the affections and feelings onto the next stage of development.

It is quintessential for parents to try and help the child to try new tasks (tasks like trying to take a walk unaided) and smile at him/her when he/she fails, this gives an affirmation of love to the kid, and then help him to try again till he/she masters the steps.

Confidence is not static, this is because as children grow, they encounter tougher challenges and these challenges build more confidence in them.

It is worthy to acknowledge the difference in children's personalities and how this can affect their confidence, that's why confidence may be easier to build in one child while the other may have to pass through strenuous patterns to attain confidence. Children who have high confidence may be faced by things that can reduce the rate of their confidence.

There are many ways a mother can help build her little child's confidence, some are explained below:

- Love your children: this is the first step to building confidence in your children, you have to love them, show them that you really care for them. By doing so, they develop a comfortable niche around you, they tend to share everything about them with you. When love is shown to kids, they tend to be open and will never keep a secret away from you. Extend this love to their friends and everything they do, when they so some good, hug them and praise them accordingly and when the outcome of their actions turns out to be a mistake, pat them on the back and motivate them to try harder next time. When a mother shows love to her kids, it becomes the foundational element that builds confidence in those children.

- Help your children learn and do new things: a child's mind has the capacity of learning new things at every stage of their development, kids learn to walk, talk and relate with their environment through a conscious systematic process. As a mother, it's a good thing when you help your kids learn new things and not just learn them, teach them how to go about them. Through this, you are teaching them how to solve problems on their own. When you teach your kids about things they should know, they gain mastery and proficiency in them. This will greatly build a lot of confidence in them. When helping them, show them how to do it, then allow them to do it themselves, if they make mistakes, leave them and correct them where necessary, this will increase the rate of their confidence. However, be sure not to teach your kids quick fixes to life approach, they may be caught aback and reduce their self-confidence

- Praise your children where necessary: when your kids perform a task successfully, it is needed as a parent that you praise them and give them necessary applauds for the success. This will spur them to want to do more and achieve more. When a child successfully performs a task, he seeks to find a response from those he loves, and this response is praise. Praising them is crucial to building their self-confidence and it pushes them to do more. As a parent, you must also learn to praise struggles and efforts, when a kid is showing signs of letdown in a particular endeavor, if it seems as if he/she has failed, you must be appreciative of the relentless efforts he/she has put into it. Probably your kid is not too good in a sport or a teamwork assignment, try and encourage him/her by telling him how great his efforts were. By doing so, you build self-reliance and confidence in him. However, you must guide against over praising your kids. What do I mean by this? When you know your kids have not done anything or have not ushered any effort but you keep praising them, that will lead them to being lazy which in turn will reduce their self-confidence.

- Be a good role model: children have the ability to study their environment and develop a character or way of life through it. When you as a parent puts efforts in every area of your daily activities, you are setting the best example for your children to follow. Kids are motivated by what they see and they develop a culture around it. Parents should be very observant about what they do in the presence of their kids because they have a way of assimilating those actions. When you as a parent clean the rooms, clear the sofas and set it well, a kid will see this and will not err from it. This will help build the confidence of the kids. Also, as parents you must model love, love yourself and the people around you when you do this you create a sense of love and affection in your kids towards the family and the society at large. When you do well at a task, praise yourself, when you do this you consciously build good confidence in your kids.

- Educate your kids never to give up: the road to success will always be rough; there will be ups and downs, only those who are willing to strive through this phase of life will succeed. Help your children to know that at some points in their life, they will experience disappointment or a particular misfortune, but that they must never let their guards down. It will be too preposterous to say life will bring to our table everything we want or will become, we all have to strive for it. Let your kids know that there will always be depression and that people will criticize their approaches to life, it may seem they have gotten to the end of their lives, make them understand that they can overcome these only if they do not give up. Teach them to try and try and try and even if they fail, they should still try again, by doing this you are teaching them resilience and resilience builds self-confidence and belief.

- Be supportive of their passion: children always have what they care about, what they are passionate about, when you try and find out these things in your children; be ever ready to support them. Don't force your own opinions on them; if you do you have caused an imbalance in their ability to trust in their own self-esteem. As a parent, encourage and respect the passion of your children, be supportive of their vision, help them achieve the feats and praise them when they do, by so doing their confidence is built. If your daughter finds interest in playing soccer support her even though you want her to be a ballet dancer, don't always force your will into your children's lives, it will reduce the confidence they have in themselves. However, supporting the passion of your children doesn't mean you are carefree towards them, or that you give them the liberty to do anything they please either good or bad. You must also learn to restrain them in love when they are trying to err.

- Give your kids the opportunity to try helping other kids out: when your kids are trying to help other kids either in school or in the community, allow them to do it, don't ever restrain your kids from helping other kids out. When they do they build more confidence in themselves. Children have a way of connecting themselves and when they do they show themselves what they can do and how they can be of help to each other.

- Help them build the right relationship skills: the foundation of all relationships starts from the family. When the relationship in the family is right, kids will emanate the traits and then extend them to society. A child must be taught to know that he/she owes others a duty of care and that he/she is also responsible to others and not just the family. You must let your kids understand that their actions affect others and they must be courteous in the way they behave to others. You as a parent cannot always be there for your children; that is why you have to teach them to be kind, intelligent, assertive and confident to handle the issues of life.

- Engage a rule setting model: As much as it is good for you to give your children their space, it's also needed that you set rules through which they are guided. Let your kids know you are in charge; don't just let them do whatever they want whenever they want to. Set rules to help manage their time, their resources and even their friends.

Life situations are based on rules, if your children cannot obey your set of rules there are high tendencies they may not be able to obey other rules set by other people. As they grow older they understand the importance of priorities because they've learnt to live by the rules. Kids who live the early stage of their life disobedient to rules may end up being delinquents later in life. When kids obey rules it gives them a sense of self-confidence and protection.

ENJOYMENT OF THE NEW ROLE

Having gained the confidence to build the right relationship between her and her children, the mother must also learn to flow consistently in this role.

The responsibility of raising children into decent adults is not one which stops in a day, it is a continuous line of action and mothers should find delight playing this role perfectly well.

Communication with little kids can be stressful, annoying and time-consuming but mothers must learn to love the process because any nonchalant attitude towards the development of children can mar their chances of being responsible adults.

Therefore, mothers should take communication in child development as a significant tool for building a responsible human in children and put all their efforts to seeing that their kids are responsible to the family, society and the world at large.

HOW TO TALK SO YOUR CHILD WILL LISTEN

Over the years, I have learned just one key fact about managing and taking care of children; they never want to listen and they do not see any wrong in what they do. I have seen that yelling at them or shouting unnecessarily at them is like making myself look like I do not know what I am doing. By doing this, it makes them more unready to pay attention to whatever I have to tell or share with them.

Just like adults, kids have lots on their minds, from their exams and tests to their next school, to trying out for soccer, reaching out to their friends for the next big party in the neighborhood, to going on dates, and getting the newest gadgets around. It is even important to add that they have to undergo lots of rewiring by age 6 and age 12 to fit in with some friends and add some newer. It is all understandable that they feel overwhelmed by stimuli and give less priority to parents. In short, parents can be seriously low on their list. This is because parents are majorly interested in making them follow instructions, listen to guides and do this or that while they are most concerned about how to explore this and see what those adults said is not right. They are most concerned about tearing things down than they want to build.

I remember when Mrs. Nathan came to me for consultation, she said ‘my daughters are ignoring me. I could tell them more than three times to do anything- like get dressed, turn off the TV, brush your teeth or even prepare for school- they either don’t listen or they don’t pay attention. Sometimes, I yell at them and threaten to throw their blankies away. This is not the parent I want to become but they are not helping matters. I feel powerless and always down when I remember I need to make them do some chores. But I’m not a disciplinarian, I do not want to turn into one, I need to get my kids to listen to me without resorting to yelling, nagging, reminding or punishing them. That is reckless and control-less parenting.' She lamented.

I understood exactly what she is going through. I have seen parents enter my office to seek how to groom their kids over and over again. They all have the same problem; getting on the same page with their kids of age one to five, who are naturally not ready to give their parents, time and attention.

In my many sessions with parents, I have seen that they are all seeking the same thing from their kids- attention. Children naturally ignore them and it is as frustrating as much as it is tiring repeating the same things over and over again.

In one of my numerous sessions, a woman told me of how her 6-year-old boy loves playing while she is making him a brief and fast breakfast. Often, they need to beat the traffic or she would end up missing her staff meetings which commence every day by 8am. She mentioned how she would call him from the kitchen to come and eat, even though she can see him sitting on the living room floor not far away. Amazingly, he would not respond. No matter how many times she called, he won't respond. Naturally, patience is worn thin and frustration boils over, she storms into the living room many times to forcefully bring her son to the kitchen for his breakfast.

- Are you having these same issues with your child? They fail to respond to calls or cautions.
- Do they feel adventurous and want to see the end of something you know is risky and hazardous?
- Do they act like they are here when their mind is elsewhere?
- Does it feel like you can't seem to control them?
- Does it look like their focus is not on what you say or direct them to do? Playing while you need them to do little and simple tasks.

- Does their inquisitiveness land you in trouble with the neighbors? Like them trying to practice things they have seen in the movies.

- Have they broken things that you can't even start recounting or accounting for? The shoe rack, the hangers and probably the dresser mirror.

If your kids display any of these behaviors, you need not to worry. Most of what they do or have done is not because they are mentally disturbed. Instead they are in that stage where they are willing to try newer things, see the connection of some electronics, look for who is speaking in the radio or even unscrew the bicycle's tire.

No! They are not having a mental exertion; they are only expressing all the possible variables in their mental workings. And the truth is, all kids act like this. Most of what they do are the most interesting to them, not the boring, lame and archaic communications. If you care to notice, you do not have to teach them how to act deaf or not respond or do what they do, this is because it is easy.

We therefore need to establish the first fact that kids find it hard to understand why their parents should be seeking to disrupt their fun. They think that their parents are kill-joy who major in coming to stop their fun when they are in the middle of it. This has caused the major issue in Parenting and Guidance- attention. The kids do not want to give it and the parents want it by all means. This has caused a predicament of attention grabbing parents who seek to grab the attention of their children by all means because they feel like they are ignored by their kids.

The first way to win the battle with your kids is to GRAB THEIR ATTENTION not CATCH their attention. Do not seek to catch their attention. Kids have other things to think about. They have their own issues, as trivial as it might look to adults, and they don't understand the importance of taking their bath or eating breakfast.

I don't pride myself for making time for my daughter or giving her enough chance. Instead, I have only embarked on some nine steps which worked like magic for me. At first, connecting with my kid wasn't easy, just like Mrs. Nathan, I felt scared, disheartened but I took time to look into what was happening with my daughter and I saw that I needed to exactly pinpoint how to make her listen. This made me develop these nine steps that worked for me. These are not suggestions but proven facts that reverberate with every kid and their parents.

Step one: GET THEIR ATTENTION

Of course, many parents love sitting their kids down to 'talk sense into them' (like Mrs. Nathan told me she did). This makes the kids lose great entertainment (yea! those kids want to watch the next Knickerbockers and it is the same as you keeping up with your favorite TV show). It makes them listen half-hearted and deaf. They suddenly turn the normal talk into a ted-talk session.

Ohhhh!! Another boring long talk. To worsen matters, no matter how you do it, there is no guarantee that they will listen to your explanations.

In my situation, I realized that kids know what they are supposed to do; they just need simple reminding. They know that the electric cooker is on and it will be hot but they still need a reminder of how hot it is.

I always tell parents that it is important they really find a common ground with their children before speaking. This means that they should connect before speaking. Speaking to your children is not a board meeting or an employer-to-employee meeting. That means you can't bark orders from across the room and expect to get through.

Finding a common ground for both of you to have a productive conversation is the beginning of hitting the right spot with your kid. You need to get down on your child's level, touch him lightly. You need to observe what his attention is focused on and use it to get his concentration shifted to you.

Making comments like “Phew! I didn’t know cats can run like Tom” will obviously make him ask questions about cats from you. It has been proven that when we feel connected to another person, we are very open to their influence. It makes it easy for them to listen to you. That is not manipulation. It is called Acknowledgment. Acknowledgment that you give credence to what he is doing but you need to make him see other things that are also important.

Getting attention doesn’t mean you quickly force the conversation to continue. You simply nudge him till he looks up. That’s the indication that what you said has caught his attention. When he looks up, look him in the eyes and start talking.

Sometimes, some of them are so into what they are doing, watching or making that they really don’t want to stop to listen to you, it shouldn’t be a source of worry. Instead what you do is to have his attention by asking “can I tell you something?” it will naturally arouse his interest and make him ready to listen to what you have to say or share.

It should not be a surprise when your kids use this technique to get your attention. It means you have great kids who would grow up to become fine gentlemen or ladies. Kids who feel a strong connection to their parents always have a strong desire to respond to their requests. To have your child listen, you have to focus on building their relationship first.

To make your children love reading or do what you need them to do, you need to take the first step with them. Make them read by reading with them. Play with them to learn their turn-offs, hassle and struggle with them, laugh with them. Wash teeth with them to make them understand the reasons for oral health. Do things first to show them the importance of doing what they do.

Connect with your kids, not impose your will.

Step Two: UNDERSTAND THE CONVERSATIONAL TRENDS

My constant sessions with parents have revealed that most parents do not win the first battle with their children before trying to talk to them. Your children will not suddenly develop listening to you because you are their parent. They will only listen to you when your connection to them is strong.

When Michelle wouldn't respond to her parent, they brought her to me for therapy. I noticed that her attention was far away from her mother and her mother hadn't discovered her conversation trend. She was always withdrawn from talks when her mother spoke forcibly. It made it hard for her to understand.

After therapy, I told Ms. Norris, Michelle's mother that she needs to discover Michelle's conversation trends. No child is withdrawn; it is just parents who have made no effort into seeing exactly how to make a grand entry into the world of their child.

Having the full consciousness of the conversational trends will help remove reasons for making continuous demands back-and-forth. It will no more be "Michelle, you need to sit still" but "Michelle, wouldn't it be great if you sit with me for a quick chat?" Kids respond to affirming words that comes from their everyday language.

Having the full comprehension of your kids' conversational trends will make you understand that they do not ignore you on purpose. If you have asked once and not gotten a response, don't just repeat yourself. You need to get the attention of the child. That means, you should revert to step one till you get the exact match of your child's conversational trend.

Step Three: YOUR CHOICE OF WORDS

There are those children who deliberately ignore their parents on purpose. Children are ever inquisitive and adventurous. It is an understatement that they take this to the extreme. This should explain why they won't back out even when you make them understand that what they are hell-bent on is injurious.

They really want to see what you'd say when they refuse to listen. They want to see your reaction to the insane things they do. They want to make mental notes and gather evidence as their previous knowledge on how you respond to dumb questions and what will happen if they ignore your questions.

Respecting your child as an individual is very important. You need an array of selective words that would resound and reverberate with them not words that will create a disinterest in having you around.

I got a mail from a friend explaining the situation of her children to me, she noted that her two kids, Darryl and Debby are two sides of a coin. While she has it easy with Debby, Darryl was very difficult. Darryl wouldn't even listen, no matter how she tries to make him. She has no issue with getting his attention but it is unlikely that what she ever tells him to do sank.

I booked a session with her, where we were able to discuss how Darryl reacted even when she has his attention. From her explanation, it is obvious that Darryl has no issues listening to her but won't do what he is told to do.

From what she said, I realized that Darryl had a certain set of words that would loosen him and make him respond actively to what he is asked to do. She said "I always persuade him to cooperate at the end, he stands resolute and looks at me like he didn't hear, it makes me sick and I can't live with that. Next thing I know; I'm yelling at him reminding him of how his friends make fun of him for his last performance at the last school dance party. This has always worked but I notice that he is becoming more resolute each day."

What has always worked is not the harsh words spoken, not the threats or punishment, I have seen children become more resolute rather than feel sorry for not cooperating. At the end, they become stubborner because they feel they are not part of a decision. Kids feel stifled when they are only shown that there is only one way which is right and it is not their way. They tend to devise their own way which is righter to them. Using the right words that would give them options and not brick wall them is the perfect way to start.

Four weeks after I told her to try changing the words she used on Darryl, she texted how grateful she is. Darryl now loves hearing how bad it will be if he fails to sleep earlier because he wouldn't love to be punished by his class-teacher. Now, he fancies coming to her to remind her of tucking him to bed earlier.

Your kids are not deaf, blind or dumb, they have feelings just as you. They understand what is happening but you have to know that getting their attention is not a guarantee to them listening to what you say or tell them. You have to get the right mix of words that would resonate with them.

When you know this, it won't be "If you don't put on your hat, you can't go on any more rides and you are going straight to bed." To them, they would love to see what happens if they fail to listen to what you want. It is too easy for them to be defiant. At the end, they know they will play on the emotional linkage they have with you and you will be the one comforting them.

Instead of those words that will cause both parties no reprieve, you should switch to words like "John, you can put your hat on now or after you sit out the next ride" Of course, John would think you are bluffing, but this is the beginning of the right process to do what is required of him. After he might have missed out of the ride, you can still turn to him and say "John, here is your hat, there is another ride." You won't force John to wear the hat because now you've made the right choice of words and actions to make him understand the importance of listening.

You should pay attention to how many corrections, requests or redirections you give your child. They make up how a child perceives how to talk with or to you and respond to your directions.

Step Four: WHISPER

As your frustration with the kids rises, so does the volume of noise that wells up in your mouth ready to escape. Often, parents want to avoid spanking their kids, so they resort to yelling as a way to discipline their children or vent their angers and frustrations.

In a recent study by the Wall Street Journal, three out of every four parents yell, scream or shout at their kids at least once a month. This has resulted to kids who retract and not fully express the reactions they would normally do. It is one of the causes for parents not knowing what their children are capable of as those kids are scared of falling on the wrong mood of daddy or mommy.

Raising your voice to get the attention of your child is as ineffective as trying to put a horse before the cart. There is this evil yelling brings, it ceases communication. As soon as parents start shouting or screaming, it makes children recoil into a thick shell, at the end, they go into shutdown.

How best do we solve this? The best thing to do is whisper. The idea is to get their attention in a rather spectacular way. A way that beats their wildest imagination. They have obviously made you frustrated but there is no better grand way to berate them than whispering what they have done. Children are inquisitive and curious, when you whisper, they kind of want to listen so they shut up to hear.

Kids who are yelled at may be vulnerable to behavioral problems and symptoms of depression. Yelling at children has a reactionary effect on them. First, they withdraw from the society as much as they can. They don't want to get involved with people who would just keep yelling at them. Then, their adult life becomes a shell, they do not engage in discussions quite often because they are scared of being screamed at. The extent of this damage is not known until they eventually give birth to their own children, they resort to yelling because that was how they've seen it done.

Yelling is a natural way to scar not just scare a child. At the end, you've successfully made those kids see life beyond you.

It is all natural that they make you boil inside. It is all natural that emotions will flow and make you want to scream. Perhaps they have left out some things to pack or keep? Maybe you are even stressed at work or worried about a phone call. Whatever reason for the worry, kids have a natural talent in pushing parents over their limit and the yelling begins. It is therefore very important for you to be in control of the situation and manage your emotional outbursts. They are kids and won't understand why you yell at them.

Yelling can only cause you more discipline issues and misbehavior. Parents should pay attention to the signs of their emotions running over, they can control the situation without yelling, which means there will be no guilt or discouraging your child.

When you stop yelling at your children, they will start listening more, start respecting you more. They will start telling you more and be happy talking to you and doing what you ask. Instead of yelling, create positive discipline, it will make your children well-behaved and have better mental health.

Step Five: EYE CONTACT

The first social skill to develop in every conversation is Eye contact. Teaching your kids how to make eye contact is helping them develop their social affirmation and strength. Use simple ways to teach your child how to make eye contact like asking him to look into your eyes when he requests a toy or treat.

An impotence to make eye contact during a conversation is a social deficit. It is a great barrier to your child's success at making friends. Making eye contact is a basic skill that leads to positive social interaction with others. It is the mark of a staunch social commenter.

As much as you are teaching your kids how to make eye contact, it is important that you also learn to make eye contact with your kids. To make your kids get better at whatever you want them to do. You need to tell them not to shield from making eye contact.

You should identify skills that you can practice with your child. Skills such as participating in conversations and making eye contact are at the top of the list. Teaching them interpersonal skills makes it easier for them to make friends and live in the society.

Help your kids to grow; make sure your child establishes eye contact when he makes requests for something. By doing this, you are teaching him the crucial link between communication and focus. No matter what he wants from you, teach them to look in to your eyes when making requests. This builds better understanding between his request and your capacity as his parent to fulfill it.

Give them practical ideas for making eye contact. You can also use visual aids to remind them to never forget making eye contact. Give them direct instructions for making eye contact during a conversation.

It is extremely important and succinctly essential that you practice what you teach your children. Instead of yelling a request or running away with passing instructions from across the room, walk over to where the child is. Get their attention before you make the request. It is important that you make eye contact. It is as affirmative as the request you want to make. Ask them to make eye contact with you, just as you do the same.

Step Six: REPEAT BACK

Ms. Adams, a neighbor, in one of our numerous sessions, painted how uneasy it is controlling her three kids.

Our family mornings are always marked by power struggles. They will never remove their toys or breakfast markers. There are always unfinished science experiments at the balcony and tiles. I naturally enjoy multitasking, so it never occurred to me that I needed to give orders to them to effect the cleanings until some weeks ago. I ended up barking repetitive orders to them. “Remove your shoes off the cushion.” “Why are your shoes still there?” “Your shoes should be removed.”

Most times, I find myself tripling my heart beat rate, my jaws clenched and my emotions tipping to burst. I did my best not to yell but I have my fair share of madness. There were those times I actually did. There were power struggles over nearly everything; getting dressed real quick, cleaning up their toys, putting their shoes on, closing the door gently.

I made plans for the next day but it never made my kids listen. All that ever happened was me making repetitive orders before action happened.

Just like Ms. Adams, most parents need to realize that spending at least 10 minutes each day doing a child-directed activity of their choosing improves kids listening. This will improve bonding and conversations between parents and children. The ten minutes are not just for doing the activities alone but to make the children know exactly what is expected of them. I call it the EXPECTATION CHAT.

I also encourage parents to empathize with their children. It is not easy to do those chores as children. They find it hard-work. In order to make them do what they are to do, I encourage that parents break down children's chores into fragments. It will encourage them to listen real quick.

To effectively stop repeating yourself, consider asking your kids when they will complete the chores required of them.

You don't need to keep repeating their duty lines every day. Instead, ask questions "when are you going to get dressed?" "How long will it take you to remove the cobwebs?" Children love escaping time, so they will set times that will make them complete the tasks earlier than expected.

Step Seven: SHOW RESPECT

Nothing shuts down communication like negativity, blaming and finger-pointing. It is important children know how to act in a civilized society. There is bound to be backlash and judgments of other parents when your son or daughter snaps back at people and others.

In a world where disrespect is now the order of the day and unending drama of no courtesies, how can children be taught to be respectful? Not just respectful to you as the parents but to other kids and others.

It is important that you need to take the first step in making your kids learn the use of respect and how essential it is. This means that you respect your kids just as you are expecting them to respect you. Study has revealed that when you respect people, you put them in a situation where they are bound to give you the same maximum respect you give them. For starters, it is a win-win situation. It enables you impart how you want your children to behave with you and outsiders. This strategy will demonstrate respect for your kids and also foster autonomy and reduce power struggles at home.

Learning to use words that depict respect is the first way to kick start respect. Ordinarily using the word please might look a bit constraining to you but for those kids, using please will teach them the universal importance of adding persuasive words to their conversation.

Respect starts from how you allow them make some decisions for themselves like when they choose to talk to you about their issues and challenges. Instead of "how was school? Or "where are you now?" try "I sure miss you when you are at school. My favorite part of each day is when you are home." It makes them open up on those things that they have faced throughout their day. It also places you as one who respects their space and is ready to give them the chance to tell you as much as they want.

Step Eight: CONSEQUENCES

Encourage your kids to follow the rules by using positive reinforcement. If there are negative consequences for breaking rules, there should be positive consequences for adhering to rules. The reward and retributive system.

Learn to give your child kudos and praise for following rules. Say something like "Thank you for doing your chore list when you got home, today. This is a surprise and

I appreciate it." Give your children plenty of positive attention to reduce attention-seeking behaviors.

As a parent, you should not just give 10 minutes for learning how to make your kids do their chores, devote time to have one-on-one time each day to motivate your child to keep up the good work.

If there is a behavior problem with your child, create a reward system. Reward systems can help turn around behavior problems fast. Kids love to earn rewards that will be shown to their mates. You might need to capitalize on this to change some bad habits they have.

Give your child warnings to know exactly when to stop an act. Use an "if" to tell the child what the consequence will be if he doesn't listen. Yelling creates a power struggle. Instead use words like "if you don't pick up your socks now, then you won't be able to play with your Play Station after dinner."

Importantly, keep in mind that you can take away electronics for like 24 hours or a week or assign extra chores to a child who break rules. It will help the child think twice about breaking the rules again.

I always don't want any kid to face the 'grounding rule.' I see it as the last punishment for any child to undergo and I have always told parents during sessions that they should never contemplate grounding their children unless the need necessitates it. And I recommend a maximum 24 hours grounding as anything beyond that is teaching the child to become errant.

Step Nine: SOLVE THE BIGGER PROBLEM

If you have done the whole eight steps and your child is still having issues connecting with you, then there may be an underlying reason for the child not listening. You need to observe the child and notice when they follow (understand) you well.

Importantly, you need to also check yourself. You should watch if you are not going too fast with your kids. It is very difficult for them to process when you stuff them with much instructions and commands at a go. Children will naturally struggle with transitions, therefore give warnings and allow for time between activities. It will aid your children break down activities real fast.

I recommend that parents use charts, lists, timers and pictures to give instructions to their children. It is naturally uneasy to teach children orally, images store better in their sub-conscious, hence the use of visuals.

Every child is a great listener, it just depends on the communication pattern between them and their parents.

Observe yourself over the next few days. The patterns and habit you have, directly imparts on your children a whole lot.

THE BRAIN OF THE TODDLERS

There is a lot to learn about the brain of your toddler. In one word, it is simply amazing. As a new mother, it may seem like there is so much you need to know about your dearest one. This is true. However, it can be a more relaxing and beautiful journey for you as long as you have the right knowledge about how they think and act, but more importantly, how this phase is most crucial to the rest of their lives.

There has been quite some research on how toddlers think and why they act the way they do. This is worth studying as they can sometimes come out as totally different people from all we have seen and admired in the movies. Basically, toddlers are all fun and more. You can, by knowing how their internal organs function, be able to raise them into becoming fine individuals that you would be most proud of in the future.

According to research done along these lines, what a child achieves in his first three years in terms of cognitive abilities, would take about sixty years or more for an adult to achieve. This is because as an adult, our sense of reasoning and absorption of both facts and abstract elements are well advanced compared to a child. In other words, the toddler's brain works totally differently from that of an adult. From about age two till age six, there are a lot of marked differences in how things are perceived and assimilated in comparison with later years.

Many theorists have thus, described the brain of a toddler as a sponge - and rightly so too. This conclusion is based on the point that they take in an enormous amount of information from the environment and the world around them. What happens in the case of toddlers is that they absorb everything in their environment. It is worthy of note that the rate of this absorption is indiscriminate, continuous and effortless. By saying it is indiscriminate, clearly shows that a toddler does not select what to absorb and what to leave out, he or she takes in just about everything. Unlike the adult that can point to what not to allow in, the toddler takes them all in. This absorption is continuous too. This means that it continues all through this very delicate stage of their lives. Then, it is equally effortless. They really do not exert any effort or force at it. After all, they are either laughing, crying, having fun, playing around or something like that. There is not really a serious moment where you can point to as the time when they are absorbing per se. Even if there are times when they are glued to the TV, it surely does not last for long before their attention moves to something else. But you see, all this while, they were absorbing so much without them even knowing. Little wonder it is so effortless!

In essence, toddlers relate with their environment far differently than adults do. They do not just see things and recall them afterwards, they absorb them; such that what they see becomes part of their very core. This is all natural to them.

Another thing worthy of note is that toddlers develop a very large per cent of their core brain structure between ages 0 and 5. From ages 0 - 3, children tend to absorb information both unconsciously and unknowingly. This is typically called the unconscious stage. This is the stage where they learn to sit, to stand, to walk, to use their hands and even to speak. They do all of this through mimicry. That is, these basic faculties are developed through mimicry. Toddlers will naturally imitate what they see; as they grow up to begin to make more independent choices. This early stage is so crucial for toddlers to move on to more complex stages of growth, or better put, more advanced stages of growth.

There are behavioral patterns exhibited by toddlers that show off how they think. These impulses are stimulated by neurons which are controlled by the brain. Hence, they are worth studying. Asides the fun that a toddler brings to the table each day, they typically engage in approximately 57 billion struggles called power struggles every day. Again, this behavior is normal and totally essential for appropriate development of the child. There are some practical things to focus on to be able to relate with the brain of a toddler and help them live out this period of their lives. Note that certain facts to be discussed here will be most valuable in knowing how to get your toddlers to learn through the process of their growing up.

The first thing to note is that toddlers, because of the level of formation of their brains, do need you to tell them a lot of times what you need them to do. This already gives off the truth that handling toddlers needs a great dose of patience, and tons of extras in your handbag, in the kitchen, the dining, everywhere!

As adults, we have what is called "executive function skills". These set of skills are responsible for our ability to focus our attention on something. It is also what is responsible for our being able to remember whatever instructions we choose to retain. It is the same set of skills that is responsible for how we control impulses. Needless to say that even as adults, we sometimes are not able to hold our emotions together, how much more toddlers who have not yet developed these skills at all. This is the reason they need to hear the same instructions over and over again. For example, a child can begin to color the walls because he or she is trying to have fun. That action may not be good for mum and dad as they have to incur some damages later. Now, telling a toddler that he or she should stay off the wall once can never do the trick. How can it? He or she does not see the reasons to stay off, nor can they - until you keep telling them again and again while letting them know that you are not happy about their actions (we shall get to that shortly), then, they can begin to step back.

Someone used the illustration of the Grand Canyon. On one side is your toddler who really wants to color the wall, on the other side is why he or she should not because of the effects it might have. Getting your toddler to see reasons why he or she should not make a mess of the wall, just like getting to the other side of the Canyon would be no small effort. Imagine building a bridge that long and more importantly, strong enough to get over to the other side!

Basically, this is what your continuous use of words, telling your toddler the same thing over and over again is seeking to achieve. One trial cannot do the job, certainly not with the bustling impulses within them; impulses that they have little or no control over at this stage.

It means you would have to tell them to keep off the wall a thousand times over (or hopefully less), for them to begin to even consider it! It would take a lot of time, which in this case is a lot of words to build the bridge and help them find the connection; that they need to keep off the walls (you know you would have to provide an alternative for them anyways, where they can actually color).

So far, the point for the new mother is to see her toddler as having very vibrant and active impulses that the child cannot control just yet. However, by repeating the same things to them again and again, you are helping them in many ways. First, they can see that anytime you correct them, the look on your face may be disapproving. As they keep noting this with each time you correct them, they will eventually be able to stay off because mum said not to, and more vividly, because they do not want to see that look on her face.

Another angle to view this is that toddlers learn better through experiences. It would take a lot and that actually is true, a lot of life experiences to successfully create the connection you seek in your toddlers' brain.

Lastly, these connections made possible through experiences is what would lead to the formation or development of the executive function skills in the toddler when they age. To reiterate, repetition is not only important but helpful for your toddler. It would require patience to keep at this. The rewards are great for your toddler. The happiness would be tremendous for you too because the intent of raising a child is for him or her to grow up a steady and complete human. Hence, it is key to remind your toddler. It is essential to guide and comfort them. This is because every single experience would help to build the bridge which they all need at this tender stage of their lives.

What then happens if a mother loses patience along the way? It is crucial to ask this question because it is true that your toddler needs the experience to learn. However, it is also true that you need the patience to allow them to go through such experiences sometimes at the detriment of your clean floor or dining table or walls.

So, when tempers are almost up on your side as the mum, just take a deep, deep breath. Another thing that can help is for you to picture the Grand Canyon and visualize that your words are truly laying more and more boards across.

There is something else to call your attention to - your toddler feels negative emotions like adults do. Feelings like anger, sadness, anxiety, powerlessness, frustration, confusion, and so on. What is different is that the adult brain now knows how to handle these situations (although the mode of handling this may differ across different individuals, yet alone if they are successful at it).

In essence, toddlers do not have the capacity of stopping to think over before taking their actions because that part of the brain that allows them do this is not yet developed. They will, with time, but for now, they will pretty much show forth any and whatever feeling that takes central stage. Like, when they feel any negative emotion, it takes over them completely. These feelings, even for your toddlers could be quite raw, new, and even confusing - so they need you more at this time, to help them.

How then can a mother help her precious one when the negative feelings come rushing in and take over? One way to do this is to put words to the feeling. Another way is to label their present emotion. You could use a reflection or mimic their expression. Mimicking their expression is a good way to get their attention at the time. For example, if your toddler is stomping his foot and refuses to stop, you can also begin to stomp yours and keep an expression on your face similar to what is on his. Then when his eyes are on you, take a deep breath - this would encourage him to take his too. So, you are helping him breathe by breathing. After which he is now calmer to hear you talk. You can then say something like, "you seem to be angry, what was it you wanted?". Also, by putting words to their emotions, you could, for example, when your toddler begins crying uncontrollably because you cut his cheese in half when he wanted it full, simply say the words that his emotions are carrying. You can say to him "okay, I am sorry, you wanted your cheese whole and I split it in half. Okay, when you are calmer, I will give you a big hug and then we can talk about it". Something around that basically.

The scenarios above can typically be called toddler tantrums. This is described as a situation where "all hell is let loose". Permit my use of that term. What happens to your toddler's brain at this point is that the lower part of the brain, particularly, the amygdala, takes over. The amygdala in this case, hijacks the upper brain region that works for decision making, morality, empathy amongst others. An example could be when you are bathing your dearest toddler and he gets upset that you poured water on his head. He begins to scream and throw things around, swings his fists and is virtually prepared for a fight! At this point, what is happening is that his stress hormones are all up and his emotions (like was said earlier) have taken over him. No part of the upper side of his brain is fully functioning or at least strong enough to control the lower part.

Needless to say, there is no point trying to explain yourself at this point. It always doesn't work! What can help is to rather, validate his emotions. What this does is that it will make your toddler know that he is actually being heard. And truth be told, everyone loves being heard. So, to help your toddler, validate his emotions and allow him calm down. When he is calm, you can then help him see why it is important to pour water on his head when bathing. What you are doing is to help him build the connection between pouring water on his head and the reason/importance of the action. Now, validating their emotions would be essentially by words. You can choose what to say but the essence should not be to prove you are right (at least, not at that moment), but rather to show that you understand what they are feeling. Let it be about them for that moment, try to relate with how they are feeling. This is because they cannot yet reason out why you did what you did; this is simply their reaction to a negative emotion felt due to an action done with good intentions. That means that toddler tantrums are very natural for toddlers. What you do during the process, as a mother is very important to validating that emotion, which is the best thing to do at the time. Afterwards, when tensions are down, you can prove your actions were right and the best for them.

Another very basic thing about toddlers is that they are in perpetual motion. Except while they are asleep, you would hardly find them seated in one place for a long time. Even when their favorite cartoon is being aired, it could keep them glued for some time, but sooner than later, they are up and about again.

We can put it this way then, toddlers are explorers, and heedless ones at that. They are ready, in their minds and subsequently by their actions, to take on the world - even though they have no clue what that actually means. Interestingly, this is exactly how they are supposed to think; there is absolutely nothing wrong with this mindset of theirs at that stage of their lives. It comes naturally to them. Toddlers are naturally curious and adventurous at the same time.

Furthermore, with all the description of the toddler already given, one thing stands out: for them to learn, they have to be allowed to make mistakes. No need trying to protect them from everything. Of course you should keep one eye perpetually on them (if you can afford to), but to box them in a corner without the freedom to explore the world around them isn't helpful at all. They need the adventure and the lessons to be gotten from there. This would help build their self-confidence and also the willingness to take initiatives later on in life. Suffice it to say therefore, that mistakes are part and parcel of the building blocks for the proper growth and development of your toddler. Mistakes are embedded in the natural process of your child's growing up.

As a mother who loves and cares about raising her child properly, you would have to allow your toddler just about enough freedom to make and own their mistakes. It goes into simple things like when your child decides she wants to put on polka dots and plaids or insists on wearing rain boots when it's all sunny outside.

The fact remains that toddlers are never judgmental about their actions. They are also not self-conscious about their decisions. They would gladly act without thinking through

-which is what some mothers wish they could at that stage. But the truth remains that they are not adults yet! They certainly have to act their age and enjoy the process until they outgrow it.

This means that, because your toddler has this amazing brain that has some things not yet developed in it, there is no fun nor gain in trying to over-correct or control them. Why this action may seem like relieving you of extra stress, it is actually doing more harm than good to your child. Among the effects that being overly corrective or controlling is that your toddler begins to feel bad about himself or herself. Moreso, this would result in shame as they would feel like they cannot get anything right.

What this also means, when mothers attempt to over correct or control their toddlers' actions is that they would be getting a lot of "no". This could lead them to get frustrated and somewhere in their subconscious, they begin to feel they cannot do anything the right way. So, while you don't want to deal with the extra mess, go late for an appointment or keep repainting your walls, your toddler needs to grow by being allowed, to a reasonable extent, to figure things out themselves. For them to learn and grow normally, they necessarily need those trial and error moments.

As a loving mum, one of the things you can do is to always learn to ask yourself, at every point when your toddler wants to do something you consider funny, "what is the worst thing that can happen if she does this"? That would help you step back a little and allow them when the consequences would not be grave to them or you. Also, you can develop a mantra to say to yourself when you are getting impatient or nervous at their "weird" decisions and tendencies. A simple mantra like "she needs this to grow well", "he needs to learn through this", "he/she has to make his/her own choices to own them afterwards". While you keep a watchful eye, allow your toddler live this stage of their lives the best way.

Penultimately, your toddler needs you to be firm but yet truly kind. A mother has to be firm to protect her toddler from harmful situations. Like I said before, there are times when you ask "what is the worst thing that can happen if I allow her do it her own way"? This question is very important as there are clearly, times when you have to be firm on instructions. For example, you are out with your toddler and about to cross the road. She sees a shiny penny on the floor and leaves you to go get it. That could have a dangerous effect. At that time, she was acting based on impulses without thinking (typical of a toddler).

In essence, because of the level of development of the brain of your toddler, a mother needs to keep her child safe. This means you can set limits for your toddlers on matters regarding their safety or even proper etiquettes. For example, you must let your toddler be clear on the fact that she has to hold onto your hands when crossing the road, no matter what she sees. You also need to tell her that it is wrong to throw off her plate of food across the floor at dinner time. Hence, while toddlers need a level of freedom to make mistakes and learn from them, a mother must be firm where necessary and be kind in the process too.

However, in the event where your toddler has taken an action beyond the limit you set, in correcting her, begin with asking her why she made that decision - this is allowing her own up to her actions. Then, kindly explain why you set the limits in the first place and why safety is important.

Lastly, the brain of a toddler does not relate well with instructions that carry 'don't" or "stop". Instead of saying "don't run", just say "can you walk slowly?". By saying "don't", it puts them in a state of confusion as they have to figure out what it is they are to stop and what they are to do instead

CONCLUSION

The emphasis of this whole book has been for new mothers to know and develop patterns that would allow for their kids to listen to them when they talk. Mothering is a beautiful experience. It has both joys and then the not so joyful moments. During delivery, your bundle of joy comes out amidst several tears or efforts (both of yours and his/hers). Raising this beautiful gift into a responsible human would take efforts too. This kind of effort must be deliberate and focused in order to produce the right results.

We have seen, as is true, that toddlers are typically impulsive. Children between ages 1 and 3 have a lot going on, and much more, a lot of formation yet to be developed in their brains. A typical example would be the executive function skills which is responsible for thinking and processing decisions to know cause and effect before they are made. Toddlers are yet to develop such skills. Little wonder you would find yourself referring to a lot of their actions as childish and impulsive - that's just typical of them.

Making your toddler listen to you would require that you speak in the language they think and relate with things at this age. One practical example that was given is the use of "don't" and "stop". If you would ever have your toddler listen to what you say or even understand the instruction you give, avoid those two words. Toddlers do not relate well with them as they are going to have to unravel what you want them to stop and also figure out what they should do instead. This example typifies the need to know and understand specific language styles adopted from Montessori's works which are very useful in helping you get along with your toddler just fine.

Basically, a lot has been said to equip the new mother for her dignifying responsibility. Foremost on the mind of any mother is that, what you do or do not do may affect the proper growth and development of your child. That means nothing can be left to chance. Take the example of wanting to "outsmart" your kid by saying "no" whenever he or she asks to do something fun or appealing to her at the time. As many times as a parent says no, in a bid to control the child's actions or limit damages around the house (you definitely can relate with what I mean here), so often does the child begin to develop in the subconscious, the opinion that he or she cannot do things right on their own. This could have very far reaching, and most important, negative consequences in the future. We have seen that a better, healthier action would be to set important limits but allow your child explore and make mistakes.

By implication, mothers need to exercise a lot of patience. I had jokingly said you would need tons of extras in practically every room and in your handbag too. But this is a truth that ought not to be exchanged. Your child needs you to help him or her. Your toddler needs you to be both firm and kind and patient with him or her.

As you seek for them to understand that you love them, and that your actions towards them are with good intentions, it is vital you understand the stage where they are in. It is the stage where they can seldom appreciate your act of love and care. A toddler will cry and throw a fist simply because mum poured water on his head in the bath. He or she could throw the entire food across the floor because mum cut the cheese in half. Actions like this from your toddler should not be interpreted as your child frustrating your efforts or trying to get you mad, but rather it is a product of what I would like to call (an emotion take over period). The lower part of the brain overshadows the action functions of the upper part and that is why they seem to be so emotional and uptight. This is totally normal for them as we have seen so far.

Hence, it would be best to practice more breathing exercises when you want to lash out at them. They have to know that you are open to hearing them out when their behavior appears impossible. One very important rule is to be around to guide them, keep them safe, but allow them try out the choices they make. As long as these choices would not harm them, allow them make their mistakes, as it is proof that you believe in them and that they can actually do some things right. All this takes place in their subconscious. It will allow for them to grow in a healthier manner, better than being over corrective or overly controlling of their actions.

Finally, toddlers hear more of what your actions suggest to them than what your words say. Little wonder you have to keep building the bridge to connect with them through your words. Just like it has been stated in the book, toddlers need you to tell them again and again, what you want them to do or to stay away from. In essence, the Montessori approach to raising toddlers is more of a connective, toddler - friendly and an approach that involves knowing how the brain of your toddler works.

The ultimate goal is to find an equilibrium between the right atmosphere that your toddler needs to grow and then how you can make this atmosphere possible using the most efficient techniques. Assuredly, putting to practice the knowledge from this book will help you raise your toddler to become a responsible human. Most importantly, your toddler can enjoy and fully explore this stage of his/her life because mum knows how to handle his/her tendencies and manage it all effectively well.

Remember, it is a journey that would require consistent efforts on your part - no matter how messy it gets and the mistakes made, it will be all worth it at the end.

Made in the USA
Middletown, DE
04 May 2020

92373767R00106